Cloud Computing: A Guide for IT Leaders

by

Dr. Zeeshan H. Khan

ISBN-13: 978-1732410107

i

Table of Contents

Introduction

In an era of increased global competition, IT organizations have strategized to find new operational models to survive and thrive as innovative leaders in the marketplace. The need for innovation that, in turn, reduces costs and increases the efficiency of IT services, has led to the creation of a variety of tools including process automation, virtualization, and, more recently, *cloud computing* (Chang, Walters, & Wills, 2013; Mazhelis & Tyrväinen, 2012). The latter of these tools—and the focus of this book—has thus emerged as a cost-effective, viable solution to the increasing needs of IT leaders that presents both financial and technical benefits. Indeed, from 2010 to 2015, IT leaders who leveraged cloud computing in small- and medium-sized organizations saved an average of $1 million in IT services for their organizations (Lacity & Reynolds, 2014; Sobragi, Gastaud Macada, & Oliveira, 2014; Yoo et al., 2012). With a background in global data storage management, I have seen firsthand how integral cloud computing can be to the business—almost all products that the leaders in my company build, develop, and sell interface with one or more aspects of cloud computing. IT leaders in my organization also leverage cloud computing services to host our internal applications.

Due to the use of cloud computing services in my organization, I had the experience of working with cloud computing infrastructure, mainly as a consumer of cloud computing services. It is here, and through subsequent research, that I realized that some barriers to utilizing cloud computing exist. In a recent study, for example, Aleem and Christopher (2013) found that 93.8% of IT leaders considered IT security and 61.1% considered IT governance as major barriers to cloud computing adoption.

Moving to the cloud computing infrastructure may also cause attenuations in staff in the organization, highlighting the need for increased investment in marketable vocational training. In this book, I unpack the concept of cloud computing to address these barriers directly, creating a how-to guide, of sorts, for IT leaders who wish to increase the competitive advantage in their organization. First, however, before entering into this discussion, in the remainder of the Introduction, I explain briefly the concept of cloud computing along with the evidence-base on which this book is based, my doctoral research, and provide an overview of the book as a whole.

What Is Cloud Computing?

Cloud computing has different meanings to different individuals. Everyday consumers view cloud computing as a standard service available through an Internet-connected mobile device (Fernando, Loke, & Rahayu, 2013; Sultan, 2014). In contrast, IT professionals view cloud computing as a pool of shared resources accessible through computing environments (Mazhelis & Tyrväinen, 2012). In sum, it is both of these things: With a foundation of server and desktop virtualization, cloud computing is a mode of shared resources at the application, data center, and infrastructure levels (Neumann, 2014). Overall, cloud computing allows IT department managers to change their outdated perceptions of IT as merely cost centers into business enablers and innovation powerhouses (Trigueros-Preciado, Pérez-González, & Solana-González, 2013). Cloud computing also enables IT leaders to defer their capital expenditures and leverage operational spending to support IT operations (Nanath & Pillai, 2013).

IT professionals are in an extraordinary position to counsel users on cloud computing because of their acquaintance with both its technical and business implications (Neumann, 2014). Traditionally, IT-supported companies functioned as an operational unit: however, now the role of IT has changed to become a strategic business enabler (Neumann, 2014). Still, cloud computing's adoption has often been slow because some IT leaders require additional assurances on user adoption concerns including security, performance, and interoperability (Dan & Chang Chieh, 2010). These IT leaders also needed to understand the paybacks pledged by this disruptive technological innovation to align technological innovations to company profitability (Dan & Chang Chieh, 2010).

And yet, the importance of reducing costs in IT operations encourages IT leaders worldwide to innovate, and various global IT leaders are leveraging innovative approaches to minimize overhead costs associated with IT infrastructures (Mauch, Kunze, & Hillenbrand, 2012). IT leaders believe that the IT infrastructure in a utility model reduces cost and leverages commodity support services (Choudhary & Vithayathil, 2013; Mauch et al., 2012). However, it is difficult for IT executives to justify investments in the new infrastructure and staffing because the indirect impact of IT offers challenges to quantifying without proper tools and chargeback mechanisms (Mauch et al., 2012). When IT leaders attempt to drive the cost out of their business to increase profitability, the cost centers are the first on the target list (Mauch et al., 2012). By leveraging cloud computing, IT leaders can add value to their business while leveraging the economies of scale resulting in improved business practices (Nanath & Pillai, 2013). As such, throughout this book, I show how cloud computing can create success for any IT organization, by identifying the barriers to adoption and suggesting recommendations to address these barriers.

An Evidence-Based Guide

This book combines recent literature on cloud computing with primary research to create a current, evidence-based resource for IT leaders. This primary research, the qualitative, single-case study I conducted during my doctoral work, focused on the strategies IT leaders use to adopt cloud computing in their organizations within a single organization in Long Island, New York. More specifically, I worked with 15 IT leaders who had a working knowledge of cloud computing strategies and who had successfully implemented at least one cloud computing initiative within the last 2 years. Using a qualitative approach, I examined these strategies from the perspective of the IT leaders, capitalizing on and gleaning from their expertise through interviews, document analysis, and participant observation.

These leaders represented various departments including application development, infrastructure, networking, operations support, vendor management, and finance. The scope of this study also included IT infrastructures, which consisted of software, hardware, communications, and facilities needed to support IT infrastructures. The IT infrastructure leaders used unique technologies that helped improve IT efficiencies and were available in the past 5–8 years. The documents reviewed included policies, guidelines, and technical whitepapers internally published by the organization related to cloud computing implementation.

It is important to note, however, that despite the robust data provided through this study, it was limited to IT leaders within the organization, not the organization as a whole. I also excluded the staff reduction elements or any elements that may have adversely affected staffing levels. As such, utilizing this methodology narrowed the findings to one geographical locale, though they hold implications for IT leaders nation-wide.

Framing Concepts

To create a sound theoretical foundation for the study, I utilized disruptive innovation theory (Christensen, 1997) as the basis for my work, which is based on a series of mature technological innovation studies (Christensen, 2011). In sum, this theory can be used to assess the efficacy and usefulness of the adoption of technological innovations within the organization (Christensen, 2011; Crockett, McGee, & Payne, 2013; McMurtry, 2012). The theory can also be used to define the marketplace, and how it is leveraged by the goods and services created based on the performance profile required by consumers and delivered by IT leaders (Dan & Chang Chieh, 2010).

Christensen (2011), a recognized expert on innovation, acknowledged that disruptive innovation characterizes an innovative model of service methodology that can augment current procedures and introduce innovative industry techniques. Evolution in IT creates disruptions in traditional business methods (Dan & Chang Chieh, 2010). IT leaders thus need to acclimate to the swift changes in the enterprise environment to stay competitive (Arora & Nandkumar, 2012; Dan & Chang Chieh, 2010; Russel & Millar, 2014). Disruptive innovation theory recognizes that sustaining innovations generates growth by offering better performance in existing markets (Christensen, 2011). In my study, I employed disruptive innovation theory to provide a basis for

5

understanding the opinions of IT professionals, as well as to observe concerns that affect consumers' adoption and tolerance of cloud computing (Dan & Chang Chieh, 2010).

In this Book

In this book, I provide a guide for IT leaders to understand and therefore adopt cloud computing processes successfully, drawing from the evidence-based literature as well as the findings from my doctoral research. This book holds great relevance for business leaders, as understanding strategies for the adoption of cloud computing will help to gain the operational and technical efficiencies of innovative technologies, resulting in cost savings as well as acceleration of time-to-market for product and services development initiatives. Accelerated time-to-market will, in turn, lead to a competitive advantage for these organizations. Furthermore, as cloud computing redefines the way IT leaders conduct business, such adoption may open new markets for IT leaders to conduct business (Andersen, Gupta, & Gupta, 2013).

In Part I of this book, I provide a foundation of knowledge for IT leaders to understand cloud computing in context, along with a set of key concepts vital to adopting cloud computing successfully. More specifically, in Chapter 1, I unpack the elements of cloud computing, including its applications, innovations, relationship to competitive advantage, and constituting elements. In Chapter 2, I move to a discussion of how to assess cloud computing, relating to performance, interoperability, flexibility, and data security. Next, in Part II, I shift from theory to practice, presenting the findings from my primary research with IT leaders who have successfully adopted cloud computing. In Chapter 3, I outline the methodology used for the study in more detail, before reviewing the findings themselves in Chapter 4 on strategies for effective cloud computing adoption as well as barriers and critical factors to implementation. Then, in Part III, I move from a discussion of cloud computing barriers and critical factors to discuss cloud design and management. In Chapter 5, I review cloud design considerations in various contexts. I also discuss the hybrid cloud solution as well as theoretical and physical design considerations, before examining cloud management and its elements in Chapter 6. Lastly, in the closing chapter, I discuss the applications of this evidence base, providing a set of recommendations for businesses as well as future research on cloud computing.

PART I: KEY CONCEPTS

Introduction to Part I

To adopt cloud computing successfully, IT leaders require an understanding of the key concepts that comprise and affect its adoption and implementation. In the first two chapters of this book, I provide an overview of some of these concepts, beginning with the application of cloud computing in IT environments. After establishing this background information, I then discuss the relationship of cloud computing to innovation and creating a competitive advantage within the IT field, before reviewing the core elements of cloud computing. Next, in Chapter 2, I discuss some of the factors relating to the assessment of cloud computing strategies, namely performance, interoperability, flexibility, and data security. Overall, Part I provides IT leaders with a thorough understanding of the context and concepts vital to cloud computing as a whole, drawn from evidence-based literature, to provide a foundation for the development of successful cloud computing strategies in any organization. This is followed in Part II with a set of findings from primary research that identify factors essential for IT leaders to consider in practice, to further ensure the success of cloud computing adoption.

Chapter 1: Elements of Cloud Computing

The first step in understanding cloud computing is to gain a fuller picture of where, when, and why it is adopted. In this chapter, drawing from recent evidence-based literature, I discuss some of the applications of cloud computing in varying industries, along with its relationship to innovation and how it can ensure a competitive advantage for any organization. I then review some of the core elements that comprise cloud computing, before moving to a discussion of factors that affect the assessment of cloud computing adoption strategies in Chapter 2.

Applications

Applications of cloud computing vary from industry to industry as well as from workload to workload (Mohlameane & Ruxwana, 2014). Priem and Swink (2012) examined the standards, architecture, and process transparency in global supply chains by leveraging innovative technologies. The evidence showed that lack of standard information systems among different organizations creates inflexibility and inconsistency (Mohlameane & Ruxwana, 2014; Priem & Swink, 2012). The absence of interoperability and flexibility across IT systems further challenges an organization's reliance on global supply chains (Priem & Swink, 2012).

Two fundamental capabilities developed over the past 5 years are that of the suppliers of AaaS and suppliers of infrastructure for the applications used by businesses (Lango, 2014). The provisions among the suppliers of AaaS and suppliers of infrastructure have resulted in distinctive system undercurrents in supply chain systems. Demirkan and Dolk (2013) addressed issues of service science as an essential area of information systems research. Demirkan and Dolk (2013) also highlighted the various characteristics of manufacturers and customers of services-focused technology advances, as well as value-add or solution vendor mediators, systems integrators, traditional businesses, users, and government officials as observers of technological advancements of cloud computing.

According to Kumthekar and Aserkar (2012), IT is an empowering driver for a supply chain. The accessibility of logistical administration software provides a competitive advantage to consumers (Kumthekar & Aserkar, 2012). Logistics administration applications leverage the SaaS model for cloud-based procedures (Kumthekar & Aserkar, 2012). According to Mohlameane and Ruxwana (2014), IT is an enabler of an organization's agility. A distinctive belief is that superior IT venture empowers an organization to be additionally nimble (Mohlameane & Ruxwana, 2014). Nevertheless, traditional IT may obstruct administrative agility for IT operations (Mohlameane & Ruxwana, 2014).

Andersen et al. (2013) discussed the notion of cloud computing as an exciting topic for business decision makers. The promise of cloud computing to deliver litheness and rheostat expenditures through a flexible service model manufactured on a shared hosted platform appeals to business owners by adding agility to their IT operations (Li, Zhao, Rong, & Tang, 2013). Andersen et al. also explained that cloud computing has brought about a new business age where cost efficiency is the foremost objective. Andersen et al. deliberated upon the IT's capabilities presented via cloud computing, including (a) benefits to organizations, (b) commercial usage, and (c) social benefits.

11

Uchechukwu, Li, and Shen (2012) discussed the efficiencies built into cloud computing that encourage the restructuring of experimental progress procedures, quickening timelines, and cutting IT infrastructure related expenses. Preliminary applications in life sciences frequently focus on the efficient management of large amounts of data produced by the research and development progression, where cloud computing can accelerate the analysis of trial data to attain expedited results (Uchechukwu et al., 2012). Augmenting the techniques used for gathering documents from numerous sources, shared, and moved to an archive system is a unique application of cloud computing (Uchechukwu et al., 2012). A shared IT environment includes the advantage of the strict security, consolidation, automation, and monitoring of external participants (Flores, Antonsen, & Ekstedt, 2014; Hu, Deng, & Wu, 2013; Sanghyun, 2014).

Dahl (2011) argued that given the comprehensive, cross-functional, and exclusive nature of the procedure of product design, comprehension of design teams requires additional investigation by leveraging shared IT resources. Strategies to adopt cloud computing may aid future researchers in enhancing their research, which may focus on (a) internal procedures refined within the product design team, (b) macro inspirations in the product design atmosphere, and (c) the explanation of product design grouping (Dahl, 2011). Henard and McFadyen (2012) contended that, while researchers look to advance innovative technologies, IT leaders lack the incentive to conclude the significance of their technologies by classifying future applications.

Henard and McFadyen (2012) emphasized a specific stage of technology development to take advantage of innovative technological advancements: the development or emergence stage. When an auspicious innovative technology development first starts in a central research laboratory, its objective and target markets frequently appear copious but lack clarity (Henard & McFadyen, 2012). The vagueness of goals and aimed markets for products under development increase demand for innovative technologies to minimize the risk factor (Dahl, 2011; Henard & McFadyen, 2012).

Xiaolong, Mills, Znati, and Melhem (2014) proposed guidelines for energy proficient cloud computing services to promote environmental friendliness: (a) installing an appropriate non-disruptive power supply, (b) using a preemptive remote administration, and (c) employing a scalable design that acclimates to fluctuating necessities or volatile requests for resources. According to these guidelines, IT leaders must also adopt innovative technological developments and sustain consistent examination plans, and valuations of the data center efficiencies to manage IT costs effectively (Li et al., 2013; Xiaolong et al., 2014). Gibson and Kasravi (2012) evaluated cloud computing to increase production for the businesses while lessening raw material and power consumption. Ye, Yang, and Aranda (2013) also observed the usage of communal and private clouds, apprehensions around the conceived threats associated with consuming cloud resources, and the remunerations of leveraging cloud computing for resource amalgamation, ecological observation, and proficiency administration.

Jing, Ali, She, and Zhong (2013) stated that virtualization delivers secure segregation of workloads traditionally delivered by dedicated physical servers to run application workloads. In addition to this secure separation proficiency, there are generous benefits to virtualization, including ease of planning, decreasing floor space requirements in the data center, reduced laborers charge due to the simplicity of management, and reduced energy usage (Jing et al., 2013; Pearce, Zeadally, & Hunt, 2013). According to Helland (2013), the function of the IT division in any organization shifts with the organization's maturity and adaptation to advancements in technology.

In sum, cloud computing holds applications for a wide range of disciplines. IT leaders have to evolve their IT departments into user-friendly and business-enabling departments to avoid executive management scrutiny (Helland, 2013; Park & Kim, 2014). The amplified attention to cloud computing, green technologies, and subcontracting are difficulties that IT departments encounter (Helland, 2013; Pearce et al., 2013). IT leaders need to evolve their methodology of IT resources, understanding the long-term business consequences that will arise if they resist this paradigm shift toward cloud computing (Helland, 2013; Pearce et al., 2013).

Innovation

Bala Subrahmanya (2013) suggested that leadership is a dominant influence affecting innovation. Numerous scholars revealed that transformational management and leadership positively affect structural innovation (Bala Subrahmanya, 2013; Henard & McFadyen, 2012). Nonetheless, there is a lack of scholars investigating the circumstantial environments of emerging innovation (Henard & McFadyen, 2012). Innovation drives the capability of an IT leader to advance innovative products or services (Hu et al., 2013; Wang & Alexander, 2013). Innovation also drives an organization's success in taking these

14

innovative goods or services to the marketplace (Hu et al., 2013; Wang & Alexander, 2013).

Hu et al. (2013) and Helland (2013) mapped the correlation of innovation with cloud computing. According to Hu et al., the need for business agility gave birth to the innovation of cloud computing. According to "Business Models for Strategy and Innovation" (2012), commercial models and innovation management are directly related. Digital technology, such as automated commerce, collaborative web applications, and cloud computing fashion a prospect for innovative business opportunities. Commercial applications of innovative technologies are also a type of innovation ("Business Models for Strategy and Innovation," 2012; Li et al., 2013).

Heng et al. (2014) examined an assortment of innovative business developments that effective business managers use to create innovative approaches to the creation of products and services. Heng et al. (2014) and Li et al. (2013) examined numerous innovations, including the enhancements of social networks to manage talent within the organization, leveraging collaboration technology, and innovations in information management. Heng et al. also supported the importance of innovation for an organization's growth by many experts, including William Dutton, of Oxford University, Rob Bernard of Microsoft, a computer software company, and Hal Varian, of the Internet firm Google. Kun, Ming, Shaojing, and Jian (2014) deliberated on the emerging technology of cloud computing in a non-technical way and observed concerns about organizational assessments and appraisals of cloud-based architectures and solutions. The use of cloud computing enhances utilization rates and decreases expenditures and overhead of cloud service suppliers (Kun et al., 2014; Park & Kim, 2014; Sanghyun, 2014).

Global IT leaders immersed in the promised value of nearly limitless computing, network, and storage resources of cloud computing leverage these resources to create value for the consumers (Cavage, 2013; Nallur & Bahsoon, 2013). The evolving nature of cloud computing encourages service-based application to adapt to the emerging values and requirements of cloud computing (Cavage, 2013; Nallur & Bahsoon, 2013). Nallur and Bahsoon (2013) focused on the value of a distributed apparatus for such automatic adaptation by leveraging standardized enhancements and innovations.

Sakhuja and Shukla (2013) explored associations among diverse categories of Internet usage, IT alignment, and planned tractability. Usage of the Internet for communication with consumers relates to strategic tractability for small and mid-sized enterprises with more market orientation (Sakhuja & Shukla, 2013). The goals of the theory are to define the marketplace, leveraged by goods and services created based on the performance profile required by consumers and delivered by the IT leaders (Dan & Chang Chieh, 2010).

A theoretical exploration of the innovation and cost control spans beyond academic research (Christensen, 2011). This exploration also includes practical implications regarding the durable sustainability of all organizations (Christensen, 2011). Innovations and advancements in technology enable IT leaders to apply these improvements in the form of innovative technologies such as cloud computing (Dan & Chang Chieh, 2010). Garrison, Kim, and Wakefield (2012) deliberated upon the applications of cloud computing systems in an organization's IT infrastructure, which may improve data storage capability while reducing IT expenses. Garrison et al. also described the categories of service models offered by cloud services providers, containing Software-as-a-service (SaaS), Platform-as-a-service (PaaS), and Infrastructure-as-a-service (IaaS). (See Glossary for the definition of terms.) In doing so, Garrison et al. noted the many competitive rewards of economic cloud computing outlook.

Neumann (2014) also deliberated upon the use of cloud computing in various operations of business organizations in the United States. Neumann identified that the innovation enables IT leaders, to leverage their existing or familiar IT infrastructure and renovates technology into communal resources distributed as a service over one or more networks. Neumann also focused on the use of cloud computing that permits Internet consumers the access and use of computing resources such as IT infrastructure and other computing resources, including software applications.

Budrienė and Zalieckaitė (2012) examined the continuously fluctuating, energetic, and various business atmospheres that drive monetary bodies, including enterprises, to respond to fluctuations in the marketplace. According to Budrienė and Zalieckaitė, the use of cloud computing also encourages these environments to pursue unique prospects and inventive resolutions permitting (a) conservation of resources, (b) development of innovative merchandises and services, and (c) persistence on the international marketplace, which necessitates superior value and promptness of information. IT leaders of small and medium-sized enterprises can fashion their technology infrastructure but doing so requires substantial monetary resources (Budrienė & Zalieckaitė, 2012). A pay-as-you-go model may enable IT leaders of a small or mid-sized organization to eliminate the need for upfront capital requirements, to deliver innovation by leveraging cost-effective means (Wang & Alexander, 2013).

Competitive Advantage

According to Liu, Sheng, and Marston (2015), corporate leaders distinguish themselves in their market segment by positioning IT to cultivate strong IT competencies and counterattack rivals' endeavors to emulate or advance these proficiencies. Although this strategy is the warranted approach because of vigorous IT proficiencies, there does not appear to be empirical evidence proving or disproving this supposition (Liu et al., 2015). IT leaders support the nimbleness of an organization's infrastructure and appetite to innovate (Mohlameane & Ruxwana, 2014). A general proposition is that the superior investments in technology infrastructure empower a business to be flexible (Mohlameane & Ruxwana, 2014). Nevertheless, it is possible that IT leaders can also obstruct and occasionally even encumber business agility (Mohlameane & Ruxwana, 2014). Mohlameane and Ruxwana (2014) offered the proposition that organizational leaders want to grow their organizational IT proficiency and administer their IT infrastructure assets to attain nimbleness and competitive advantage.

Roberts and Grover (2012) examined how IT leaders may accelerate an organization's client dexterity and competitive commotion. Consumer demands drive the behavior of a company's leaders and encourage them to innovate to maintain their competitive advantage (Roberts & Grover, 2012). IT agility also performs a significant role in the collaboration gained from the communication amongst a company's leaders' synchronization efforts and their advancement in the integrated information systems (Nanavati, Colp, Aiello, & Warfield, 2014). These integrated information systems enable IT leaders to respond to the dynamic demands of consumers to attain competitive advantage (Nanavati et al., 2014).

Haimes and Chittister (2012) deliberated on the impact of cloud computing on organizational strategy and corporate representations. Haimes and Chittister anticipated that IT leaders, who efficiently manage threats around cloud computing, created a sustainable competitive advantage. A unique advantage of cloud computing is to enable businesses to answer their consumer requests efficiently (Haimes & Chittister, 2012). Helland (2013) highlighted the infrastructure required to support cloud computing initiatives by associating with the limitations and conveniences of living in shared housing such as apartments and condominiums. Helland also emphasized the importance of practice and presentation designs in the formation of PaaS, the progress of utility-modeled software and applications in the deployment of SaaS, and efficient applications of web-based access to shared application resources for cloud users.

Cloud computing allows IT leaders not only to alleviate threats to the highly competitive commercial atmosphere but also to advance competitive leads (Iyer & Henderson, 2012; Walterbusch, Martens, & Teuteberg, 2013). Iyer and Henderson (2012) designated numerous cloud computing advantage configurations and a few business-related tactical hazards. Vigorously handling a blend of legacy IT and cloud solutions is an IT administration necessity as businesses participate in networks that embrace rivals, infrastructure suppliers, and software platform providers (Nanavati et al., 2014).

Ussahawanitchakit (2012) targeted the effects of information attainment regarding the competitive advantage of e-Commerce industries in Thailand through technology recognition and information productivity as mediators. Information attainment is the self-governing adaptability, where technology reception and material productivity are the regulating variables, and competitive advantage is the reliant variable (Chauhan, Malhotra, Pathak, & Singh, 2012). Liu et al. (2015) searched the degree to which competitive activities of international IT leaders and local merchants of Internet merchandises and services formulate the dispersal of their corresponding merchandises or services in developing marketplaces. Liu et al. authenticated the premises with longitudinal field data from two combinations of rival Internet products in the search engine and e-markets.

Nevala, Ollila-Tåg, Pitkäkoski, Takala, and Toivola (2012) discovered how to achieve expertise in a traditional business with an innovative service. Numerous diverse materials of concern exist when introducing an innovative service to the marketplace to create competitive advantage (Huang, Wu, & Chen, 2013; Nevala et al., 2012). Nevala et al. gained this opinion from management scholars knowledgeable in the corporate lifecycle.

According to Kaur and Chana (2015), the eventual objective of cloud computing is to deliver excellent tractability where the consumer can have any source and information at any time, in any quantity, with robust safety, and custom-made service level agreements. Consumer leverages a utility model, with no upfront capital expense in a cloud computing environment (Chauhan et al., 2012; García, Espert, & García, 2014; Walterbusch et al., 2013). Timely availability of software and hardware resources is a significant factor in implementation and deployment on-demand to improve customer satisfaction and to stay competitive (Kaur & Chana, 2015).

Constituting Elements

Organization-wide adoption of cloud computing presents flexibility and enhancement over the traditional client-server model to organizations, as well as the older time-sharing models of the 1970s (Caytiles & Lee, 2012). Cloud computing delivers an economic, innovative, and traditional computing platform to greater masses at scale (Caytiles & Lee, 2012). Cloud computing enables consumers to easily access, install, and acquire innovative technologies that are traditionally cumbersome to procure and consume (Sultan & van de Bunt-Kokhuis, 2012). Cloud computing's shared service models, including IaaS, SaaS, and PaaS, apply to many cloud computing models, including public, private, hybrid, and community cloud offerings (Chao, 2014; Young Bae, Junseok, & Bong Gyou, 2013).

After the success of virtualization, many IT leaders started to build their internal or private clouds by extending their virtualization capabilities to the end users via service catalogs (Chao, 2014; Garg, Versteeg, & Buyya, 2013). These virtualization capabilities included server, network, and storage virtualization (Chao, 2014). These internal or private clouds require in-house capabilities to support all the components of the cloud (Frey, Hasselbring, & Schnoor, 2013).

By leveraging existing infrastructure components to create internal clouds, benefits the IT leaders to reduce their cost of entry into the private cloud model (Young Bae et al., 2013). If using existing infrastructure is not an option, IT leaders also offer commercially available private clouds to their organizational users. Internal or external services providers host and manage dedicated clouds (Frey et al., 2013). Leveraging private clouds enables IT leaders to consolidate their infrastructure assets (Lal & Bharadwaj, 2015).

Shared or public cloud computing models take advantage of combined cloud resources for more than one organization or business (Lal & Bharadwaj, 2015). Commercial cloud providers manage and host public clouds, including hyper-scalars such as Amazon, Microsoft, and Google (Lal & Bharadwaj, 2015). End users lack any control over the services and underlying infrastructure (Young Bae et al., 2013). Services offered by public cloud computing providers are *pay-as-you-go*, or subscription based. Customer-relationship-management (CRM) systems such as Salesforce.com are effective examples of how customers consume public cloud resources (Lal & Bharadwaj, 2015).

Hybrid and community clouds are an amalgamation of public and private cloud model (Chandrashekhar, Gupta, & Shivaraj, 2015; Goutas, Sutanto, & Aldarbesti, 2016). Community clouds leverage communal resources to serve many IT leaders who form a community because of their common trepidations, duties, and purposes (Katzan, 2010). Community clouds include a combination of internally as well as externally hosted resources (Katzan, 2010). The hybrid cloud approach combines the private, community, and public cloud approaches into a single model (Katzan, 2010).

The hybrid cloud models leverage the interoperability as the minimum common factor between private, public, and community approaches (Chandrashekhar et al., 2015; Goutas et al., 2016; Katzan, 2010). Hybrid clouds require internal as well as external infrastructure investments. Hybrid clouds enable IT leaders to control their mission-critical data and applications while leveraging the scalability and flexibility of internal and external cloud computing resources (Chandrashekhar et al., 2015; Goutas et al., 2016). Cloud computing service providers offer these services in the form of bundles to attract consumers and to provide users with the flexibility of choice and economies of scale (Katzan, 2010).

Cloud services models such as a SaaS enables customers to operate their applications out of cloud infrastructure (Lal & Bharadwaj, 2015). Consumers access the SaaS applications via a web browser over the Internet (Katzan, 2010). In a SaaS environment, the consumer does not have access to the underlying infrastructure and can only make selective modifications to the applications themselves.

Some of the SaaS offerings include CRM, virtual servers, and desktop applications, where communication methods include messaging, and numerous others (Lal & Bharadwaj, 2015). The cloud-computing infrastructure delivers messaging, including email and instant messages because of their Internet dependency (Lal & Bharadwaj, 2015). Management of messaging consumes numerous internal technical resources; therefore, messaging is a candidate for outsourcing to the cloud (Lal & Bharadwaj, 2015). Outsourcing messaging has its caveats, including the risk of data loss and ownership issues, including sensitive information sharing among the employees over messaging (Lal & Bharadwaj, 2015).

PaaS allows consumers to customize the application, perform application development tasks, and leverage application development methodologies supported by the cloud provider (Lal & Bharadwaj, 2015). PaaS offerings include application development tools and environments, databases, and web services (Goutas et al., 2016). PaaS offerings do not allow consumers to have access or permissions to alter the fundamental cloud infrastructure that supports the PaaS offering (Chandrashekhar et al., 2015; Goutas et al., 2016). PaaS environments enable additional controls for the end user in the application environment as compared to a SaaS offering (Lal & Bharadwaj, 2015). Some of the examples of PaaS include Microsoft Azure and Google Apps (Goutas et al., 2016).

IaaS enables the usage and management of cloud computing software resources, including services such as computing and networking capabilities, virtual machines, and virtual storage pools (Rahman & Choo, 2015). The IaaS offerings usually include (a) physical domains, (b) virtualization, and (c) networking (Rahman & Choo, 2015). The IaaS enables customers to consume virtualized computing resources in a *pay-as-you-go* or utility model (Rahman & Choo, 2015). IaaS models empower consumers to leverage IT infrastructure resources without incurring any capital expenditure (Katzan, 2010). The end user can administer and modify the software layer of the infrastructure, including data storage space, network resources, and operating environments (Chandrashekhar et al., 2015; Goutas et al., 2016). Some of the IaaS offerings include Microsoft Azure, and Amazon Elastic Compute Cloud (EC2) available to consumers (DaSilva, Trkman, Desouza, & Lindič, 2013; Goutas et al., 2016).

Organizations such as Amazon, Google, and Microsoft evolved into popular cloud services providers for organizations of all sizes and provided a utility model for consumption of their cloud resources to their consumers (Karadsheh, 2012; Thanakornworakij, Nassar, Leangsuksun, & Paun, 2013). Cloud providers such as Amazon, Google, and Microsoft leverage the economies of scale methodology and achieve higher returns on the total cost of ownership of their cloud underlying resources by increased hardware and software resource utilization by leveraging a multi-tenant resource consumption model (Karadsheh, 2012). Enterprise-grade cloud services providers typically offer both *pay-as-you-go* and leasing options to their consumers because the trend of resource consumption varies from client-to-client (Karadsheh, 2012). IaaS providers leverage the secure multi-tenancy consumption models to enhance their resources utilization (Zissis & Lekkas, 2012). IaaS providers prefer to leverage applications, computing, network, and storage resources that allow them to leverage multi-tenancy and to be scalable (Zissis & Lekkas, 2012).

Multi-tenancy enables cloud providers to achieve economies of scale by pooling their cloud resources in a shared pool and delivering resources to the end users as a service (Zissis & Lekkas, 2012). Secure multi-tenancy comprises secure isolation of resources at the computing layer, network layer, and storage layer (Zissis & Lekkas, 2012). Examples of best-of-breed multi-tenancy solutions include VMware's server virtualization at the computing layer, Cisco's network virtualization at the network layer, and NetApp's storage virtualization at the data storage layer.

The secure multi-tenancy model leverages load-balancing and secure isolation of workloads in the cloud infrastructure (Zissis & Lekkas, 2012). Load balancing enables users to scale-up or scale-down the usage of cloud computing resources without running into any resource contention (Zissis & Lekkas, 2012). A secure multi-tenancy feature of shared cloud resources makes these cloud resources consumable by the consumers in a secure manner (Zissis & Lekkas, 2012).

Cloud computing scalability and flexibility take advantage of the speedy network, internal local area network or external wide-area network, cheap and dense data storage and high performance virtualized computing farms running on powerful microprocessor technology (Alali & Yeh, 2012). Innovations in networking, data storage, and computing platforms facilitated the rapid growth in cloud computing advancement (Zissis & Lekkas, 2012). Virtualization enables IT leaders to use different operating systems and applications in cloud computing (Pearce et al., 2013).

Economies of scale play a vital role in IT leaders adopting virtualization to extend the utilization of their physical IT infrastructure resources (Mazhelis & Tyrväinen, 2012; Pearce et al., 2013). Virtualization of IT infrastructure resources was the catalyst for cloud computing (Pearce et al., 2013). Virtualization enables IT leaders to adopt and consume innovative technological advancements with minimal lead-time for deployment of resources (Bugnion, Devine, Rosenblum, Sugerman, & Wang, 2012). Virtualization technology vendors are aligning their hardware and software innovative developments to the developments in cloud computing to improve their operational and technical efficiencies that result in the acceleration of their business growth and competitive advantage (Alali & Yeh, 2012).

Cloud computing vendors are using virtualization to extend their physical IT resources, including high-performance computing, clustering, and load balancing to the cloud services consumers (Mauch et al., 2012). IT leaders of large organizations such as Microsoft, Exxon-Mobile, and Apple use virtualization technologies to improve efficiencies of their data centers (Young Bae et al., 2013). Some cloud computing providers use hardware focused systems while numerous others leverage network-focused methodology to the deployment of network and computing resources (Mauch et al., 2012).

The marketplace includes choices of cloud computing platforms and providers for organizations. According to Young Bae et al. (2013), numerous enterprises' IT users use data storage, data management and backup, and network related services in the cloud. Cloud computing platforms integrate with the traditional application platforms (Giessmann & Stanoevska-Slabeva, 2012). Nonetheless, unavailability of integration with numerous homegrown applications concerns IT professionals and hinders the adoption of cloud computing (Lai & Yu, 2012).

Summary

In this chapter, I discussed the application of cloud computing in various contexts. As a diverse practice, such applications range between industries and workloads. The innovation embodied in cloud computing has set it apart as an effective approach for business managers and IT leaders; increasing the organization's innovation has been shown to increase its capacity as a whole. As such, cloud computing has been shown to be consistently beneficial to organizations and helps to increase organizations' competitive advantage within an increasingly global marketplace. It also holds benefits for the larger community, such as increasing energy proficiency and improving economic aspects. Finally, cloud computing's shared service models (e.g., IaaS, SaaS, and PaaS) can be utilized in varying applications, including public, private, hybrid, and community cloud offerings, and have varying virtualization capabilities. It is thus essential for IT leaders to understand throroughly how to identify the most effective cloud computing adoption strategy for their organization to ensure success. In the following chapter, I further discuss some of the factors that help IT leaders to assess the viability of a cloud computing adoption strategy.

Chapter 2: Assessing Cloud Computing

Now that the applications and elements of cloud computing are established, it is helpful to unpack some of the aspects that should be considered in adopting a cloud computing strategy as identified in the evidence-based literature. These aspects can be considered as key factors that, when reviewed in relation to the specific context of the organization, can guide the assessment of a cloud computing strategy for IT leaders. In this chapter, I review four of these factors: performance, interoperability, flexibility, and data security. Combined with Chapter 1, this discussion provides the foundation of knowledge required to move to a more practical discussion of cloud computing adoption in Part II.

Performance

The performance of resources in cloud computing environments is an important factor that IT professionals should consider before deciding if a cloud platform is a good fit for a certain application or workload (Benedict, 2013). The performance encompasses the latency, availability of Input/output (I/O) operations and response time of the workload (Tan & Teh, 2013). Without scalability of performance, cloud-computing platforms cannot meet the needs of current workloads and applications (Benedict, 2013). Technical terminology in IT for performance reflects the capability of the IT leaders to fulfill a request promptly or respond to a query promptly (Lin & Chang, 2013). Performance can also relate to the satisfaction of human necessity in a prompt fashion (Mauch et al., 2012). The components of cloud computing components scale for performance and capacity (Benedict, 2013). Performance scalability enables IT leaders to extend the usability of their hardware, software, and storage components (Mohlameane & Ruxwana, 2014).

Automation helps with the scalability of performance in a virtualized or cloud environment (Benedict, 2013). Performance factors enable the elasticity in cloud computing infrastructures by delivering features and functionality to applications quickly, reducing their time-to-market (Katzan, 2010). Automatic load balancing for performance is the main attribute for federated cloud computing infrastructures (Mladenow, Kryvinska, & Strauss, 2012). One of the concerns of IT leaders is that the commoditization and utility models of cloud computing services may lead cloud services suppliers to lessen the required performance levels (Mladenow et al., 2012). Another concern is the availability and the response times that the consumer applications require for their optimal usability (Mladenow et al., 2012). The geographical diversification of cloud computing resources also impacts the response times and performance of cloud computing services (Young Bae et al., 2013).

The availability and reliability of cloud computing resources also affect the performance of a cloud-computing platform (Katzan, 2010). Availability of resources signifies the user's desired level of access to cloud computing resources and reliability deals with the accuracy of information or data requested by the end user (Mohlameane & Ruxwana, 2014). Reliability often reflects the sturdiness, elasticity, and recoverability of a cloud-computing platform (Clarke, 2012). Lack of reliability causes adverse results for the organization, such as data corruption and loss, which results in operational inefficiencies (Clarke, 2012). These operational inefficiencies result in loss of market share, as well as loss of profits for the organization (Katzan, 2010).

Interoperability

Interoperability denotes the capability of innovative technology to be reliable and compatible with existing or old technologies (Young Bae et al., 2013). IT leaders, who embrace cloud computing, face challenges, including security, interoperability, and restrictions on the adaptation of enterprise resource (Abouelhoda, Issa, & Ghanem, 2012). The propagation of cloud computing presents issues with interoperability, transportability, and relocation of data and resources (Sultan, 2014). Interoperability is also a challenge for in-house applications, but this issue magnifies in cloud computing environments (Poulymenopoulou, Malamateniou, & Vassilacopoulos, 2012). In an in-house model, IT leaders manage their infrastructure and platforms at any time internal IT leaders can make any change or improvement (Young Bae et al., 2013). The cloud provider manages and controls the infrastructure, where consumers do not have any control over the underlying infrastructure (Young Bae et al., 2013).

Interoperability is a vital factor in the acceptance of IT innovations in corporations, but as a model, interoperability is restricted to methodological or serviceable influences (Poulymenopoulou et al., 2012). Interoperability is also important due to the correlation of the value of interoperability among the business and the embrace of IT advancements (Sultan, 2014). The reduced uncertainty of any innovative technology translates into the better adoption of that innovation by the potential consumers (Li & Li, 2013). Interoperability of a cloud computing platform influences the adoption rate of that platform as well

31

(Li & Li, 2013). Increased interoperability and openness of a technological novelty encourage cross-platform development (Li & Li, 2013).

Ease of use is a byproduct of cross-platform compatibility in cloud infrastructure (Huang, Chen, Chen, Hsu, & Hsu, 2014). Lack of compatibility with other industry practices and standards creates gaps in the production readiness of a product (Huang et al., 2014). Standardization generates ease of integration, ease of management, and ease of development for the end users and improves the time-to-market for the products and services under development (Huang et al., 2014). Mission and culture of an organization play a vital role in the alignment of technology infrastructure and business objectives (Huang et al., 2014). Lack of business values and IT alignment causes failure of many IT projects (Jeon, Min, & Seo, 2014). A useful innovation encourages teamwork over isolated methodologies (Jeon et al., 2014). In a business environment, the cloud platform's integration points with the organization's existing culture and infrastructure drive the success or failure of cloud computing initiatives (Nadjaran Toosi, Calheiros, & Buyya, 2014). IT leaders look for compatibility in a cloud platform as an important factor while evaluating those platforms (Nadjaran Toosi et al., 2014).

Flexibility

Environmental influences such as socioeconomic, administrative, lawful, and technological elements influence businesses to be adaptive and flexible. IT leaders use several tools to monitor and control these environmental fluctuations (Barrett, Howley, & Duggan, 2013). IT leaders who do not embrace change tend to lose their innovative and competitive advantages

32

(Barrett et al., 2013). International laws influence how global IT leaders conduct their business across borders. Narayanan (2012) discovered that a rationalization exists in prevailing international law for republics' cloud computing regulations to have an extraterritorial consequence. Narayanan also revealed that collaboration produces a superior malleability for the governing body and permanency for cloud computing. Cloud computing enables flexibility and cost control for data storage, resulting in additional economic capabilities (Mazhelis & Tyrväinen, 2012; Onsongo et al., 2014).

The movement of innovative and legacy applications to a cloud-based platform necessitates adapting these legacy applications to an innovative computing standard (Andrikopoulos, Binz, Leymann, & Strauch, 2013). Andrikopoulos et al. (2013) emphasized the importance of leveraging virtualization to transfer the entire application stack to a cloud platform, allocating the essential workforce resources to work on innovation enhancement. Advancements in technology-enabled cloud services have to be adaptable and flexible for data and application migration (Andrikopoulos et al., 2013).

According to Nassim Aryani (2014), IT leaders have to emphasize their competencies in the incorporation and integration of information systems and to deliver the suitable information systems that align with organizational goals, therefore, gaining the competitive advantage in the global economy. This competitive advantage requires the adoption of dexterity in the business (Nassim Aryani, 2014). Nassim Aryani also stated that the technological advancements forecast the adaptive proficiencies in the business. Technological advancements further enable the

33

attainment of business objectives, elasticity, answerability, and enhancement of the excellence and productivity in an organization (Nassim Aryani, 2014). Innovative technological advancements including cloud computing enable IT leaders to excel and achieve flexibility and accelerate adeptness. Customization and integration of cloud platforms enable IT leaders to attain a competitive advantage by being able to speed up servicing of their users and partners (Manias & Baude, 2012). Measurement of the awareness of IT leaders on malleability is an integral element in the cloud adoption decision-making process (Manias & Baude, 2012).

Data Security

Finally, data security is perhaps the most vital element in the cloud adoption decision-making process because of numerous security and data ownership concerns. IT leaders keep their sensitive data and intellectual property securely behind firewalls to deter hackers and unauthorized access (Flores et al., 2014; Sindhu & Mushtaque, 2014). Cloud computing includes new concerns and challenges around the protection of data and software applications, including confidentiality of personal information, as well as protection of the physical and virtual infrastructure resources (Desai, 2013; Srivastava & Kumar, 2015).

The Internet has global economic, political, and social impact, where strict regulations do not always govern the use of Internet resources (Sindhu & Mushtaque, 2014). Use of the Internet to enable cloud-computing resources to the public generates various uncertainties about the data security in cloud computing (Desai, 2013; Flores et al., 2014; Srivastava & Kumar, 2015). Juels and Oprea (2013) discovered the relationship between cloud

34

computing and a service archetypal that emphasizes on open and shared data security architecture. Juels and Oprea noted that corporate IT leaders' sluggishness with migrating to open clouds is a result of their concerns that go past encryption of records and files in the cloud. Juels and Oprea stressed the importance of real-time checking and appraisals by neutral auditors, which can institute safekeeping perceptibility in the publically shared cloud resources to guarantee IT leaders that the cloud offering is secure.

Sunyaev and Schneider (2013) encouraged endorsement of cloud computing offerings by autonomous accreditation institutions, which may address the issue of nimble organization's disinclination to deploy this innovative technological advancement. Sunyaev and Schneider also emphasized data irregularity in the cloud computing marketplace, the absence of statistical data to appraise cloud offering's superiority, data safekeeping, and vagueness around lawful amenability with transnational confidentiality rubrics. Desai (2013) stressed the importance of innovative engineering strategies and blueprints to address information safety concerns and the development of cloud computing. The legislative and regulatory initiatives by governments around the globe offer key strategies to safeguard data and private user information in a public and private cloud, including, but not limited to, unauthorized access and use of private or personal data (Cohen, 2013; Desai, 2013; Schweitzer, 2012).

Dadameah and Costello (2011) examined the United Kingdom government's tactical and strategic progress in the information and infrastructures technology business, specifically the contribution of advanced schooling institutes. The partnerships among academics and small and medium-sized businesses reveal a healthy attitude toward inspiring inventive undertakings (Dadameah & Costello, 2011). Dadameah and Costello also considered the concerns involving the part of advanced education institutions in economic progress and the issues that both enterprises and academia have, the prevalent issue being a constructive transformation in outlook.

The use of information technologies in an organization's corporate scheme techniques is a crucial and undisputed success factor in the marketplace (Jabbari Sabegh & Motlagh, 2012). To advance administrative proficiency and to attain competitive advantage, tools such as alignment of IT with company's corporate policies are necessary (Jabbari Sabegh & Motlagh, 2012; Madhani, 2012). Jabbari Sabegh and Motlagh (2012) ascertained the influence of IT control and competencies on tactical placement amongst corporate and IT, and the magnitude of their impact.

Haimes and Chittister (2012) focused on the handling of risks and insurance for cloud computing. Gold (2012) highlighted a 2011 Cloud Hack episode that happened in the United States, where hackers hacked approximately 100-million consumer account files and penetrated the cloud site, illegally retrieved, and obtained the private and confidential account information. Schweitzer (2012) and Gold examined the concerns regarding indemnification, improved cyber-security defense expenses, and portfolio the data influenced.

Data security in the cloud is a concern for numerous IT leaders in their administrative planning regardless of the budgetary and economic benefits (Sindhu & Mushtaque, 2014; Srinivasan, 2013). Cloud computing providers have resilient motivations to design solutions that sustain

36

performance and structures while affording robust segregation and safety to maintain competitive advantages (Hyman, 2013; Madhani, 2012; Nanavati et al., 2014). Juels and Oprea (2013) positioned cloud computing as a service model with an emphasis on public cloud data security. Numerous IT leaders hesitate to embrace public clouds because of safekeeping apprehensions, as the motivations for movement is more than encryption of records and information management in the cloud (Juels & Oprea, 2013; Wenge, Lampe, Rensing, & Steinmetz, 2014). Random third-party exploration can introduce safety prominence in cloud computing environments, assuring the IT leaders that the cloud resources are safe and secure (Changsoo, Daewon, & Keunwang, 2013; Juels & Oprea, 2013).

Improved operational efficiencies are a byproduct of cloud computing innovations (Henard & McFadyen, 2012). The outsourcing element of cloud computing reduces operational overheads (Wang & Alexander, 2013). Cloud computing accomplishes business agility without sacrificing the competitive advantage of leveraging the best of breed technology (Pedersen, Pedersen, & Riis, 2013). Cloud computing also enables IT leaders to operate a lean IT infrastructure in-house and use external infrastructure building blocks to support business development initiatives (Pedersen et al., 2013). Numerous cloud providers exist in the marketplace with a variety of cloud offerings, and major players to include Amazon, Microsoft, Verizon, and AT&T. Existing literature reviews point to the scope of this study regarding the strategies that IT leaders use concerning the adoption of cloud computing for their organizations.

Summary

In this chapter, providing evidence from the recent body of literature, I reviewed four key elements—performance, interoperability, flexibility, and data security—that are vital to consider in developing and adopting a cloud computing strategy. These elements can shape and impact the viability, efficacy, success, and ease with which a cloud computing adoption strategy is implemented; therefore, it is essential that IT leaders consider these factors in any organization. Together with Chapter 1, this discussion provides a foundation for IT leaders of the essential knowledge required to review the application of cloud computing in their organizational context. In Part II, I follow this discussion with a presentation of the findings from primary research I conducted to illustrate further factors that affect the practical application of cloud computing strategies, drawing from data provided by 15 IT leaders with extensive experience in cloud computing adoption.

PART II: ADOPTING CLOUD COMPUTING

Introduction to Part II

With our new understanding of the key concepts of cloud computing, I now shift from theory to practice, to present the findings of the primary research I conducted for my doctoral research. In sum, this qualitative, single-case study explored the available strategies IT leaders in IT organizations may use to adopt cloud computing in their organizations. In doing so, I identified the most effective strategies for adoption, along with a set of barriers and critical factors that affect implementation. These findings, taken together with the evidence base established in Part I, provide in-depth understanding and a template or guide, of sorts, for IT leaders who wish to adopt cloud computing to increase their competitive advantage in their organization. In the following chapter, I present the methodology of the study in more detail, followed by the key findings in Chapter 4.

Chapter 3: The Study

In this chapter, before presenting the findings in Chapter 4, I briefly review the methodology used for the study. In sum, in this qualitative, single-case design, I aimed to address the following research question: What are the available strategies IT leaders may use for adopting cloud computing for their organizations? To answer this question, I drew from two primary data sources: interviews with 15 IT leaders and document analysis. The documents included standard operating procedures, policies, meeting minutes, whitepapers, and guidelines related to cloud computing implementation. Selection criteria for the research design depended on (a) the research question, (b) the extent of control the researcher may have over the actual social event, and (c) the degree of focus on contemporary events (Yin, 2014). A case study is appropriate when (a) the research questions concern *how*, *what*, and *why* inquiries; (b) the researcher does not have control over social dealings; and (c) the focus is on current events (Yin, 2014)—all features of this study.

Population & Sampling

The participants of the study were IT leaders who had experience with designing and deploying cloud computing solutions at an organization located in Long Island, New York. I used purposeful sampling strategy to select the participants, which involved the appropriate selection of participants based on specific characteristics of population size, selection criteria, and knowledge of the area (Kipkulei, 2013; Sinkovics & Alfoldi, 2012; Yin, 2014). The participants consisted of 15 IT leaders of at least 18 years of age who had been working in the IT profession for 5 or more years, and who had successfully implemented cloud computing within the 2 years before the study. The participants represented various departments, including application development, infrastructure, networking, operations support, vendor management, and finance. The participants were accessed through the human resources department of the organization, which permitted me to contact staff members involved in the adoption and implementation of cloud computing.

Data Collection

As stated above, I used two main data sources: semi-structured interviews and documentation. The interviews with the IT leaders acquired data from their experience regarding their observations on the elements of their IT infrastructure impacted by cloud computing adoption and its effects. All participants answered a set of eight predetermined questions, providing their unique views and opinions on the topic at hand. Each interview, lasting less than 60 minutes in duration, took place in a conference room of the organization, and was audio-recorded and transcribed verbatim in preparation for data analysis. Each transcript was provided back to the participant for member checking, to reduce the risk of misunderstanding and increase the accuracy of the information (Maxwell, 2013; Morse & McEvoy, 2014). The participants then verified the findings, increasing the validity and accuracy of the data for analysis (Barratt, Choi, & Li, 2011; Sinkovics & Alfoldi, 2012). Overall, the interviews provided contextually relevant and rich information that captured the participants' perceptions and the particulars of the specific case, and reduced certain bias encountered in unstructured interviews (Yin, 2014). The interviews also assisted with the exploration of comprehensive experiences (Petty, Thomson, & Stewa, 2012).

In addition to the in-person interviews, I collected organizational documents such as policies, guidelines, meeting minutes, and technical whitepapers related to cloud computing implementation from the organization. The use of multiple data sources in this way enabled the triangulation of evidence, which increased the reliability of the data collection process (Heale & Forbes, 2013; Yin, 2014).

Data Analysis

I used the data analysis strategy of pattern matching (Yin, 2014) to identify emerging themes from the data in the following logical and sequential process. First, as suggested by Cambra-Fierro and Wilson (2011), data collection and data analysis were concurrent processes in qualitative research. Second, as suggested by Franzosi, Doyle, McClelland, Putnam Rankin, and Vicari (2013), the qualitative data analysis mainly included classification of items, persons, events, and their characteristics and features. Third, the data analysis process involved developing codes and using them to classify the data (Cambra-Fierro & Wilson, 2011; Franzosi et al., 2013; Morse & McEvoy, 2014). The codes included categories pertinent to the problem statement, purpose statement, research question, and interview questions that emanated from the data (Ali & Yusof, 2011; Cambra-Fierro & Wilson, 2011; Franzosi et al., 2013). To help with the data analysis, I employed NVivo to identify themes in the interview data and documentation, and integrate the data outcomes into a narrative of the IT professional observations. NVivo also supported reflections and notes from the documentation review.

Ethical Considerations

Ethical approval was obtained from the Walden University Institutional Review Board to conduct the study (Approval No. 03-30-16-0117784). Overall, the study posed minimal to no risks to participants. Data collection commenced only after receiving informed consent from participants. All participant data was protected to maintain the privacy, confidentiality, and anonymity of the participants. The data from this study, encrypted and stored on a secure server, will be retained for 5 years after the publication of the research.

Summary

In this chapter, I briefly reviewed the methodology used to conduct my doctoral research, which was comprised of a study of the experiences of 15 IT leaders in adopting cloud computing in their organization. Through a combination of semistructured interviews and document analysis, the data were triangulated, and saturation was reached, ensuring dependability and validity of the results. These data were used to create the set of findings identifying the most effective strategies for cloud computing adoption, along with a set of barriers and critical factors that affect implementation, to which I now turn in Chapter 4.

Chapter 4: Findings on Adopting Cloud Computing

Following the methodology outlined in Chapter 3, a set of findings emerged based on the IT leaders' experiences in implementing cloud computing strategies. From this data, the analysis process revealed 10 core emergent themes that fell into four main categories or overarching themes:

1. The essential elements of strategies to adopt cloud computing;

2. The most effective strategies in the adoption of cloud computing;

3. Leadership essentials for adopting cloud computing; and

4. Barriers, critical factors, and ineffective strategies affecting the adoption of cloud computing.

Taken together, these findings serve as a framework or set of guidelines that can help IT leaders to adopt cloud computing in their organization. Learning from experts in the field, these findings illustrate real-word experience that reveals the intricacies and complexities of the IT environment and prepares leaders with tools and knowledge vital to the successful adoption of cloud computing. In this chapter, I review each of the four overarching themes, presenting supporting evidence from the data.

Essential Elements: Data Security and Cost

Participants' responses to four of the interview questions (1, 2, 5, and 8) along with the document analysis identified two main or essential elements that must be considered for any cloud computing adoption strategy to be successful: data security and cost. This finding was consistent with the literature (Andersen et al., 2013; Jabbari Sabegh & Motlagh, 2012; Madhani, 2012; Neumann, 2014). Juels and Oprea (2013), for example, positioned cloud computing as a service model with an emphasis on public cloud data security, while numerous others have noted the relationship between cloud computing and cost reduction (e.g., Nanath & Pillai, 2013).

First, regarding data security, as Participant 2 stated, "The first Number 1 priority is the security of the data that we do have because that is the intellectual property of the company." Participant 8 further noted, while referring to the importance of security as an essential element, "The strategies that we used to adopt cloud computing included a focus on the reputation of the cloud vendor, scalability, security, and availability." This view was supported in the organization's documentation. In the meeting minutes of November 2014, for example, the organization noted: "Security and privacy are major considerations when evaluating application and data deployment and the data being used. IT should understand compliance requirements and establish cloud deployment policies."

As the literature shows, the decision to move other systems to the cloud improves efficiencies, reduces operating costs, and increases earnings (Nanath & Pillai, 2013). It is no surprise, then, that cost was the second of the two main elements considered when adopting a cloud computing strategy. As Participant 9 stated, "We are a lean organization with a focus on cost reduction." This view, again, was supported in the organization's documentation. In their cloud implementation guide, for example, they stated:

The cost associated with hosting the application over the term of usage is a key factor when considering application and data deployment. Thorough understanding of private cloud services costs (e.g., monthly server cost) and understanding public cloud variable costs, such as outbound internet bandwidth usage, is critical to establishing an apples-to-apples comparison. The costs of developing and maintaining application capabilities in-house also need to be compared with the alternative of using off-the-shelf cloud services with an ongoing subscription model.

Most Effective Strategies

In the second of the overarching themes, participants' responses to the interview questions (1, 4, and 8) combined with the document analysis highlighted some of the most effective strategies for the adoption of cloud computing. Of these strategies, one stood out in particular and was emphasized by all participants: the hybrid cloud strategy. The hybrid cloud approach combines the private, community, and public cloud approaches into a single model (Katzan, 2010). Hybrid clouds enable IT leaders to control their mission-critical data and applications while leveraging the scalability and flexibility of internal and external cloud computing resources (Chandrashekhar et al., 2015; Goutas et al., 2016). The hybrid cloud approach also enables IT leaders to leverage their existing IT expertise and experience to make better future IT investment decisions.

In the voices of the participants themselves, Participant 2, while referring to the hybrid cloud strategy as the most effective strategy to adopt cloud computing, stated "[The] hybrid model has

worked for us, so we're going to stick with it."
Participant 7, similarly stated, "We went with a
hybrid model." Participant 2, while commenting on
their time-to-market, noted, "Our developers
develop applications faster in the cloud." Further
supporting this assertion, Participant 3 also stated,
"We develop fast in our hybrid cloud;" Participant 8
relayed, "Our hybrid cloud helped us reduce our
time-to-value;" and Participant 10 reported, "Our
hybrid cloud strategy allows us to develop fast off-
prem and on-prem." The organization's cloud
implementation guide further indicates the
implementation of hybrid cloud strategies, with
their effectiveness confirmed in meeting minutes
from December 2013, January 2014, and March
2014. Overall, all participants mentioned that the
hybrid cloud strategy had enabled their company to
leverage existing on-premise IT resources as well as
off-premise resources to meet the demands of their
new application development initiatives. Cloud
computing's shared service models, including IaaS,
SaaS, and PaaS, apply to many cloud computing
models, including public, private, hybrid, and
community cloud offerings (Chao, 2014; Young
Bae et al., 2013).

Leadership Essentials

The results of Interview Question 5 along
with the documents identified the leadership
essentials beneficial for adopting cloud computing.
Here, all participants indicated that by being a
consumer of their cloud services, they could
evaluate themselves and take the leadership stance
by being their first customers. All participants
mentioned that they regularly evaluated themselves
to improve their service offerings while also
evaluating external cloud service providers.
Participants 2, 4, 5, 7, and 8 mentioned that they
evaluated external cloud service providers by

reviewing their market reputation, financial stability, and security offerings. For example, Participant 2, while referring to the leadership characteristics they used that were beneficial in their adoption of cloud computing, indicated "You have to treat yourself as a cloud customer of your own." He continued that by treating their internal users as customers, they could conduct self-evaluations to improve their service offerings. In contrast, Participant 4 stated, while commenting on their cloud vendor evaluation criteria, "We evaluate the vendors by reviewing their reputation in news media and keeping an eye on how they are doing in the stock market." A review of the organization's vendor evaluation policies, as well as the meeting minutes from July 2015, validated these remarks.

Barriers and Critical Factors

In their responses to the interview questions (3, 6, and 7), participants identified a set of barriers, critical factors, and ineffective strategies affecting the adoption of cloud computing. Barriers included lack of interoperability of legacy application in the public cloud offering. Critical factors included data mobility and data availability, along with performance and scalability in the cloud computing adoption strategies. Ineffective strategies included the lack of having effective exit strategies while planning a cloud computing adoption strategy.

Overall, the findings indicated that IT leaders need to understand the factors that prevent cloud computing adoption strategies from being effective. Participant 10 stated, for example, "Our main concern with all of our data is security and ease of access." Participant 3 noted, while referring to their corporate email deployment in the cloud, "it is highly available." The organization's cloud implementation guide and meeting minutes from

December 2014 further underscored their IT leaders would not implement any cloud offerings that lacked data mobility and availability.

As such, the lack of data mobility and availability is a critical factor in IT leaders' ability to adopt cloud computing. Therefore, IT leaders should ensure data mobility and availability before executing on a cloud computing adoption strategy. The availability and reliability of cloud computing resources also affect the performance of a cloud computing platform (Katzan, 2010). Availability of resources signifies the user's desired level of access to cloud computing resources and reliability deals with the accuracy of information or data requested by the end user (Mohlameane & Ruxwana, 2014).

All participations further mentioned that a lack of an exit strategy also gravely influences the effectiveness of a cloud computing adoption strategy. Participant 4, for example, noted, "Let's say you weren't getting the performance that you needed for the applications in the cloud, we needed to make sure that our costumes have an exit point." Participant 8 also indicated, "I need to be able to exit the cloud if the need arises." These statements were further supported in meeting minutes from May and October 2014.

Therefore, IT leaders should incorporate an exit strategy as part of the cloud computing adoption strategy. According to Schaffer (2014), many IT leaders fail to consider an exit strategy when adopting a new cloud computing solution, because few want to consider the demise of the great solution under implementation with great determination and hope. An exit strategy is critical to plan for unexpected events, such as providing secure and economical ways of recovering and relocating data from a cloud provider if the need arises (Aleem & Christopher, 2013; Katzan, 2010; Schaffer, 2014).

All participants P1 through P15 indicated that lack of interoperability in the cloud computing environment is another barrier that prevents successful implementation of cloud computing adoption strategies. While referring to the lack of interoperability of legacy applications in the cloud as a barrier to cloud computing adoption, P4 stated, "interoperability within the cloud amongst all the different despaired hardware and software was a barrier." P9 also stated, while referring to the barriers that prohibited their cloud strategies from being successful, "The interoperability with legacy applications and making sure that the old applications as well as the new ones that are being developed worked."

A review of ABC Company's cloud computing implementation guides and meeting minutes of January 2014 validated P4 and P9 remarks by uncovering that lack of interoperability excluded numerous legacy application from cloud implementation. IT leaders, who embrace cloud computing, face challenges, including, security, interoperability, and restrictions on the adaptation of enterprise resource (Abouelhoda et al., 2012; Katzan, 2010). The propagation of cloud computing presents issues with interoperability, transportability, and relocation of data and resources (Benedict, 2013; Sultan, 2014).

Finally, all participants highlighted that performance considerations and lack of scalability of a cloud solution might hinder the successful execution of a cloud computing adoption strategy as well. For example, Participant 2 stated, "We were initially hesitant to go to the cloud because we are concerned about some performance in the cloud."

Participant 5 indicated, "The concerns about the availability, scalability, and security . . . are very important." The organization's vendor evaluation guide further supported the importance of application performance and scalability. Without scalability of performance, cloud computing platforms cannot meet the needs of current workloads and applications (Benedict, 2013). Performance scalability enables IT leaders to extend the usability of their hardware, software, and storage components (Mauch et al., 2012; Mohlameane & Ruxwana, 2014).

Summary

The analysis of the data collected through interviews with 15 IT leaders and organizational documents revealed a set of four main categories or themes vital to effective adoption of cloud computing, which is well supported in the literature. In sum, the findings revealed:

1. Data security and cost are essential elements to consider in any cloud computing adoption strategy.
2. The most effective strategy for the adoption of cloud computing is to utilize the hybrid cloud strategy.
3. Regarding leadership, by being 'their first customers,' IT Leaders should regularly self-evaluate to improve their service offerings, as well as evaluate external cloud service providers by reviewing their market reputation, financial stability, and security offerings.
4. Identifying barriers and critical factors is important to success, particularly factors relating to data mobility and availability, having an exit strategy, interoperability, and performance and scalability.

Taken together, these findings may serve as a blueprint, of sorts, of elements to consider that help to frame an organization's cloud computing adoption strategy to ensure success.

PART III: CLOUD DESIGN CONSIDERATIONS AND MANAGEMENT

Introduction to Part III

To architect and manage cloud computing successfully, IT leaders require an understanding of the fundamental concepts that comprise and affect its design and management. In Part II of this book, I discussed some of the factors relating to the assessment of cloud computing strategies, namely performance, interoperability, flexibility, and data security. I then presented a set of findings from primary research that identified key factors essential for IT leaders to consider in practice. Now, in Part III, I move to examine the significant design considerations IT leaders should review in adopting cloud computing, include the hybrid cloud solution, theoretical design considerations, physical design considerations, and service-oriented architecture. I then discuss cloud management, including service management, performance management, data management, security management, and monitoring and billing, to ensure further the success of cloud computing adoption.

Chapter 5: Cloud Design Considerations

With a thorough understanding of the factors that impact adoption, it is now time to look at the cloud design considerations IT leaders must review to ensure success in their organizations. In this chapter, I first review the hybrid cloud solution, which research has shown to be the most effective strategy for adopting cloud computing. I then discuss both theoretical and physical design considerations that are a part of adoption, before looking at the management of cloud computing in Chapter 6.

Hybrid Cloud Solution

In sum, cloud computing is an exceptionally advantageous application that shares assets on various end-points (Kumar & Sharma, 2017). There is an expansive number of clients that leverage it to get the information. The fundamental use of cloud computing is that information saved by the client is not stored locally, rather it is stored on a server farm on the World Wide Web. The consistent quality of the cloud relies upon how the workloads are being handled. Load adjusting implies circulating workload over different processing assets. Load adjusting must take into account two noteworthy assignments, (a) the asset giving or asset designation and (b) errand planning for circulated condition (Kumar & Sharma, 2017). Numerous analysts have proposed different strategies to enhance the load adjustments.

Some compelling drivers encourage organizational leaders to evaluate a hybrid cloud strategy. These drivers include the inability of existing on-premise systems and resources to fulfill the demand of new application and innovations, the unpredictable nature of existing and new workloads in the digital economy, and the inability of existing on-premise infrastructure to support the fail fast application development methodologies. Companies with an extensive application portfolio need to be able to determine hybrid cloud infrastructure requirements before starting new applications or moving existing applications into a cloud environment (Lin, Hsiao, Cheng, Lee, & Jan, 2015; Shinder, 2013). Several novel applications will have different demands in the areas of networking, storage, compute, access control, security, availability, and performance. As such, IT leaders need to determine if the public cloud infrastructure service provider they choose can deliver on the requirements they define in each of these areas (Lin et al., 2015; Shinder, 2013).

Several IT leaders have started to integrate cloud services from public cloud vendors like AWS, Azure, and Google into their existing on-premise infrastructure (Lin et al., 2015; Shinder, 2013). Several organizations have already created new roles and positions in their departments to manage this evolution of hybrid cloud data services. These new roles can be referred to as *cloud architects*, and they are typically responsible for managing the virtualization, networking, as well as storage capabilities in the cloud as well as on-premise. Cloud architects typically architect, design, and implement the cloud adoption strategies in an organization.

Theoretical Design Considerations

Theoretical design considerations or reference models are defined before any physical elements are designed to ensure a successful physical design and implementation of hybrid cloud services. High-level components of a hybrid cloud design are depicted in a reference model that is generally vendor agnostic (Lin et al., 2015; Shinder, 2013). The theoretical design may highlight generally acceptable lingo when evaluating different cloud vendor service offerings (Lin et al., 2015; Shinder, 2013). A theoretical design also clarifies its relationship with the problem domain that it was created to resolve or address.

After defining the theoretical design, hybrid cloud architectural principles may be defined. These principles will serve as guidelines for the physical design to adhere to (Lin et al., 2015; Shinder, 2013). When designing a cloud infrastructure for a blend of workload categories with stable cost structures and service levels, IT leaders need to deliberate a diverse kind of design procedure (Lin et al., 2015; Shinder, 2013). A hybrid cloud infrastructure presents novel variables, because even if IT leaders presently host a private cloud infrastructure on-premise, IT leaders are not accountable for qualifying the crucial cloud features in the public cloud service provider's supported service offerings (Lin et al., 2015; Shinder, 2013). Having a private cloud on premises is not a prerequisite for having a hybrid cloud infrastructure. In that case, IT leaders are not at all accountable for delivering any of the critical features of cloud computing, because the only cloud IT leaders are working with is the external public cloud services provider.

All the principles and guidelines of a private cloud are also applicable to a hybrid cloud infrastructure (Lin et al., 2015; Shinder, 2013). Guidelines provide overall directions and strategies to support the growth of cloud infrastructure services. They are durable, infrequently modified, and notify and support the way a cloud satisfies its mission and objectives. They should also be persuasive and aspiring in some respects because

58

there needs to be a linkage with business drivers for transformation (Lin et al., 2015; Shinder, 2013). These guidelines are often symbiotic, and collectively they form the basis on which a cloud infrastructure is architected, designed, and deployed. After defining the theoretical guidelines, IT leaders can define the principles for integrating cloud services from a public cloud provider with the organization's on-premise services and technical capabilities.

Physical Design Considerations

After completing the theoretical design, appropriate products and services are selected to implement hybrid cloud infrastructure design. The physical design considerations for a hybrid cloud deployment include: (a) authentication and directory services, (b) compute services, (c) network services, and (d) data storage services. After choosing the products, technologies, and services to implement the hybrid cloud infrastructure, the design process of the hybrid cloud infrastructure solution continues.

When designing a hybrid cloud infrastructure, the first matter IT leaders need to resolve is how to acquire and provision accounts with the public cloud service provider (Lin et al., 2015; Shinder, 2013). Also, if the public cloud service provider supports multiple payment options, IT leaders will need to select which payment option best fits their needs today, and whether, in the future, they may want to reexamine the payment selections they first selected. According to Shinder (2013) you also need to consider whether you want to have the same person who owns the account, and therefore is responsible for paying for the service, to also have administrative control over the services that are running the public side of your hybrid cloud infrastructure. In the majority of the cases, the payment responsibilities and the organizational obligations will be distinct. Additionally, IT leaders will have to determine whether their cloud service provider permits this kind of role-based access control (Lin et al., 2015; Shinder, 2013).

Name resolution is a vital action for any application in hybrid cloud infrastructure (Lin et al., 2015; Shinder, 2013). Applications that span on-premise components and those in the public cloud infrastructure provider's network must be able to resolve names on both sides for all tiers of the application to work easily with one another. Hybrid cloud infrastructure supports several options, including (a) directory support based on the on-premises DNS infrastructure, (b) directory support based on an external DNS infrastructure, and (c) directory support provided by the private cloud services provider (Lin et al., 2015; Shinder, 2013). Each of these options has its advantages as well as disadvantages.

Compute design reflections focus on the virtual machines that will be hosted on-premise and in the public cloud service provider's network (Kumar & Sharma, 2017; Lin et al., 2015; Shinder, 2013). In some cases, the only virtual machines that contribute to a hybrid cloud infrastructure are on the public cloud infrastructure service provider's network, since the on-premise resources will be hosted on physical hardware instead of being virtualized. Whether existing services are running on physical or virtualized hardware, IT leaders need to take into account matters related to the virtual machine service offerings offered by the public cloud service provider (Kumar & Sharma, 2017; Lin et al., 2015; Shinder, 2013).

In many cases, a hybrid cloud infrastructure necessitates the extension of a corporate network to the cloud infrastructure service provider's network so that communications are conceivable between the on-premise and off-premise infrastructure assets (Kumar & Sharma, 2017; Lin et al., 2015; Shinder, 2013). There are numerous principal matters that need to be considered when designing the networking component to support the hybrid cloud infrastructure. Services that are placed in the public cloud infrastructure service provider's network may need to be load balanced to support the performance and availability characteristics that are required by an organization for a hybrid application running on a hybrid cloud infrastructure (Kumar & Sharma, 2017; Lin et al., 2015; Shinder, 2013). There are numerous methods that can enable load balancing of connections to services that are hosted on the public cloud infrastructure, including load balancing options provided by the cloud vendor (Kumar & Sharma, 2017; Lin et al., 2015; Shinder, 2013).

When viewing choices for data storage in a hybrid cloud infrastructure setup, current storage practices and storage options are assessed that are offered by the public cloud infrastructure service provider. Storage issues that are to be considered include: (a) storage tiering options, (b) IaaS database options, and (c) PaaS database options (Kumar & Sharma, 2017; Lin et al., 2015; Shinder, 2013). Another vital selection to consider is the role a public cloud infrastructure service provider can play in disaster recovery and business continuity (Kumar & Sharma, 2017; Lin et al., 2015; Shinder, 2013). The public cloud infrastructure service providers typically offer several business continuity and disaster recovery options that they natively support.

Summary

In this chapter, I discussed cloud design considerations in various contexts particularly relating to the adoption of a hybrid cloud solution, the most effective adoption strategy. After classifying the requirements and restrictions in an IT environment, and then assessing each of the design considerations detailed within this chapter, IT leaders can create a hybrid cloud infrastructure design that best meets their organizations' unique needs. In the next chapter, I shift to a discussion of cloud computing from a management perspective, the final element in a successful adoption strategy.

Chapter 6: Cloud Management

Any process adopted within an organization needs to be managed effectively to be successful. As such, in the final part of the cloud computing equation, in this chapter I discuss various aspects of cloud computing management, beginning with service management and its relationship to anything-as-a-service offerings for any organization. I then review management issues related to performance, data, and security, followed by monitoring and billing of the cloud assets.

Service Management

In sum, cloud computing makes it possible to compliantly acquire, grow, and publish computer assets on-demand to support changing workloads. Stakeholders in corporate and academic sectors are progressively exploring cloud deployment options for their critical applications (Faniyi & Bahsoon, 2016; Li, Xu, Wang, & Wang, 2012). Having a service catalog is extremely important for any cloud services offering. Amazon's AWS is an excellent example of a service catalog in the public cloud. Numerous enterprises that want an "Amazon-like" private/internal cloud offering are leveraging closed systems like BMC and others as well as open source systems such as OpenStack to accomplish this goal.

The cloud computing paradigm has become a mainstream solution for the deployment of business processes and applications (Faniyi & Bahsoon, 2016; Li et al., 2012). In the public cloud vision, infrastructure, platform, and software services are provisioned to tenants (i.e., customers and service providers) on a pay-as-you-go basis. Cloud tenants can use cloud resources at lower prices with higher performance and flexibility than traditional on-premise resources without having to care about infrastructure management (Faniyi & Bahsoon, 2016; Li et al., 2012). Still, cloud tenants remain concerned with the cloud's level of service and the nonfunctional properties their applications can leverage. Recently, researchers have focused on the nonfunctional aspects of the cloud paradigm, among which cloud security stands out. Cloud services have advanced to a model of technology that is used widely, and often is the choice for new and innovative applications and services (Faniyi & Bahsoon, 2016; Li et al., 2012).

The cloud platform offers on-demand provisioning of virtualized resources and a pay-per-use charge model to its hosted services to satisfy their fluctuating resource needs. Resource scaling in the cloud is often carried out by specifying static rules or thresholds. As business processes and scientific jobs become more intricate and involve more components, traditional reactive or rule-based resource management methods are not able to meet the new requirements (Faniyi & Bahsoon, 2016; Li et al., 2012). One of the critical issues in the management of cloud-based systems is the development of a service-level agreement (SLA) negotiation framework using an intelligent third-party broker negotiation strategy. Current frameworks exploit various negotiation strategies using game theoretic, heuristic, and argumentation-based approaches for obtaining optimal negotiation with a better success rate (negotiation commitment). However, these approaches fail to optimize the negotiation round, total negotiation time, and communication overhead involved in the negotiation strategy (Faniyi & Bahsoon, 2016; Li et al., 2012).

The cloud services approach focuses on positive user experience while shielding the user from the complexity of the underlying technology

(Faniyi & Bahsoon, 2016; Li et al., 2012). Each cloud service progresses through a well-defined life cycle: The cloud service provider defines the cloud services to be offered and exposes them via a service catalog; service requesters instantiate the services, which are managed against a set of service-level agreements; and finally, the cloud service is destroyed when it is no longer needed (Faniyi & Bahsoon, 2016; Li et al., 2012).

As computing infrastructure expands, resource management in a large, heterogeneous, and hybrid cloud environment becomes a challenging task. In a cloud environment, with uncertainty and dispersion of resources, one encounters problems of allocation of resources, which is caused by things such as heterogeneity, dynamism, and failures. Unfortunately, existing resource management techniques, frameworks, and mechanisms are insufficient to handle these environments, applications, and resource behaviors (Faniyi & Bahsoon, 2016; Li et al., 2012). The characteristics above should be addressed adequately in any cloud adoption and management strategy to provide efficient performance of workloads and applications.

As cloud technologies become, more prevalent, stable, and secure, more and more companies are beginning to realize the business value of the out-of-box solution of cloud services regarding the availability, scalability, and flexibility that cloud computing can provide. Furthermore, regarding risk mitigation for business-critical systems, the need for self-healing networks is spurring on the use of intercloud solutions. According to Aoyama and Sakai (2011), intercloud solutions provide higher reliability and higher quality cloud services in case of service failures of the cloud system caused by the disaster and unexpected increase in load.

Depending on the specific business need, the service models can be offered in SaaS, PaaS, and IaaS, or a combination mashup service that provides the end user the illusion of a single solution (Jamsa, 2013). Service-oriented architecture (SOA) gives tremendous flexibility for information systems and engineers when being built or engineered. However, implementing SOA using preexisting aging equipment presents a multitude of complication and challenges. Most SOA approaches offer to rebuild enterprise information systems, which will then have scalability. The approach for SOA is to conceptualize a service-oriented technology or migrate to service modeling in a network service system. Some even perceive SOA to be at the strategic level or a low technical level because of the potential mismatch between business models (Ralyté, Khadraoui, & Léonard, 2015).

Security Management

Cloud computing provides enormous business opportunities, though it is, at the same time, a complex and challenging paradigm. The major concerns for users adopting the cloud are the loss of control over their data and the lack of transparency (Mehraeen, Ghazisaeedi, Farzi, & Mirshekari, 2017). Providing accountability to cloud systems could foster trust in the cloud and contribute toward its adoption. Assessing the accountability of a cloud provider is becoming a critical issue, not only for demonstrating accountability, but also to build it (Mehraeen et al., 2017). To this end, we need techniques to measure the factors that influence accountability.

Over the Internet, cloud computing reveals a remarkable potential to provide on-demand services to consumers with greater flexibility in a cost-effective manner (Mehraeen et al., 2017). While moving toward the concept of on-demand service, resource pooling, shifting everything on the distributive environment, security is the major obstacle for this new dreamed vision of computing capability. Security is a major concern for enterprises, and a good information security framework is essential for the continued success of enterprises that use cloud computing services with vendors (Mehraeen et al., 2017). The ISO/IEC 27002 security standard is based on a management systems approach and is the choice of many enterprises for developing security programs (Mehraeen et al., 2017). As enterprises are rapidly adopting cloud services for their businesses, measures need to be developed so that organizations can be assured of security in their businesses and can choose a suitable vendor for their computing needs.

Cloud computing is becoming increasingly popular because of its peculiarities, such as the availability on demand of a significant amount of resources, even for a long time in a secure manner (Mehraeen et al., 2017). For this reason, cloud computing represents an excellent solution for those companies that want to outsource part of their software processes (Mehraeen et al., 2017). However, cloud computing introduces new security and management challenges on traditional systems exposed on the Internet.

Hybrid cloud infrastructure also drives the overall business strategy instead of just being a cost center. As such, IT leaders must ensure that they have complete visibility into the security of their infrastructure including on-premise and in the public cloud. Lack of visibility into the infrastructure itself is considered a high security risk. It is vital for IT leaders to ensure that every hybrid cloud infrastructure asset has assigned ownership.

Monitoring and Metering Resource Utilization and Billing

As more organizations adopt a hybrid cloud strategy, they face unique challenges for managing the performance of applications, such as poor visibility and control over resources in the cloud infrastructure (Litke et al., 2007; Oliveros et al., 2012). IT leaders who are employing hybrid clouds will need to appraise the readiness of their performance management to support these new hybrid cloud environments. There is frequently a misunderstanding that 'hybrid cloud' suggests that an application (or an element of an application) are operating in two places simultaneously. At least today, this is seldom the case, although in a future that progressively embraces things like containers and microservices this dichotomy of implementation may become more of a reality (Litke et al., 2007; Oliveros et al., 2012). Another way of saying this is that there is no need to increase the complexity of the existing implementations unnecessarily. Today, IT leaders should begin with confirming that they have visibility into the end-user experience for both the public cloud and on-premise applications (Litke et al., 2007; Oliveros et al., 2012). IT leaders should use this observation to deliver early caution indicators of potential issues.

Without access to public cloud infrastructure, IT leaders struggle with ensuring the outstanding end-user experience for applications offered through hybrid cloud environments, and cloud vendors' SLAs cover only the infrastructure under their control (Litke et al., 2007; Oliveros et al., 2012). Monitoring the end-user experience from the point of consumption (the user's device) removes the restrictions confronted by other methods which necessitate access to the application code, include proxy servers or load-balancers, or which only emulate end-user experience. Monitoring and metering are essential actions for service-oriented infrastructures (SOI) and cloud services. The data collected through monitoring is essential to confirm the accurate implementation of the workloads in the hybrid cloud and the monitoring of the SLA compliance (Litke et al., 2007; Oliveros et al., 2012).

Monitoring responsibilities include an essential functionality in every cloud computing system (Litke et al., 2007). Each service should be monitored to verify its performance and permit remedial activities in case of a failure. Monitoring data characterizes a useful snapshot of the system conduct and performance in a time series. Such information is vital in determining the source of the issues or for fine-tuning different system components (Litke et al., 2007; Oliveros et al., 2012). For instance, fault detection and recovery mechanisms require a monitoring element to decide whether a specific subsystem or server should be restarted due to the data gathered by the monitoring system. Metering tasks are essential for examining the disk space, network, and memory utilization from the platforms. These data are vital to assign services to situations of optimal performance (Litke et al., 2007; Oliveros et al., 2012).

It is not insignificant to infer from the monitoring data collected from the different systems the performance of the application, and conclude if the application is performing appropriately (Litke et al., 2007; Oliveros et al., 2012). On the one hand, a comprehensive outage in one part of the network impacting a few servers inside the application architecture could not affect the performance perceived by the user, for instance during low usage period where the rest of the service platform can provide the requested performance to the user. On the other hand, an entirely efficient infrastructure could be inadequate to provide the quality of service demanded by the end-users. Therefore, the monitoring system should collect data from the infrastructure and from the application components themselves to have a comprehensive assessment of the implementation and performance of the application (Litke et al., 2007; Oliveros et al., 2012).

The perfect condition is the accurate forecasting of the user demand so that the provider can anticipate the requirements and adjust the application on-demand to support this request (Litke et al., 2007; Oliveros et al., 2012). Accurate forecasting is one of the promises of the cloud, the flexible adaptation of the application to the dynamic environment that influences it. The application must be designed ahead of time to enable the on-demand deployment and reconfigurations of applications to support these fluctuations in the core architecture of the application to achieve accurate forecasting (Litke et al., 2007; Oliveros et al., 2012). When an unforeseen fault happens that influences the performance of the application, the cloud vendor should offer the mechanism to detect those events and respond to them to curtail any undesirable effects on the end-users. From a functional point of view, the anticipated condition is when the monitoring application is capable of suggesting remedial activities to faults and measures that can affect the application performance (Litke et al., 2007; Oliveros et al., 2012).

Summary

In this chapter, I discussed cloud management in various contexts, including as it relates to service provision, security, and monitoring and metering resource utilization and billing. I further highlighted the importance of having a monitoring and metering system that can leverage predictive behaviors and patterns to perform capacity and performance forecasting, and proactive management of the hybrid cloud infrastructure. In the final chapter, I wrap up this discussion with an overview of the key takeaways from this book, along with the various applications and implications of the evidence base established in this book for professional practice and research.

Conclusion

In Part I, I unpacked cloud computing, identifying its core elements and key concepts by drawing from the evidence-based literature to provide a thorough understanding of the topic. This knowledge provides a foundation for IT leaders to strategize, develop, and implement a cloud computing adoption strategy for their organization. Following this discussion, in Part II, I presented the method and results of the primary research I conducted for my doctoral study. In sum, this research identified four key findings that should be considered by IT leaders to adopt cloud computing successfully:

1. Data security and cost are essential elements to consider in any cloud computing adoption strategy.
2. The most effective strategy for the adoption of cloud computing is to utilize the hybrid cloud strategy.
3. Regarding leadership, by being 'their first customers,' IT Leaders should regularly self-evaluate to improve their service offerings, as well as evaluate external cloud service providers by reviewing their market reputation, financial stability, and security offerings.
4. Identifying barriers and critical factors is important to success, particularly factors relating to data mobility and availability, having an exit strategy, interoperability, and performance and scalability.

After presenting the method and results of the primary research conducted in my doctoral study, in Part III, I discussed various elements of cloud computing design and management particularly relating to the hybrid cloud solution, including theoretical and physical design considerations, service management, security management, and monitoring and metering resource utilization and billing.

Implications

The findings of this research extend knowledge of the strategies that IT leaders use to adopt cloud computing first established in the literature. According to Kuang-Hua, Fu-Hsiang, and Wei-Jhou (2016), cloud computing has many benefits such as lower cost, instant access to hardware resources, and higher scalability. Liu, Yang, Qu, and Liu (2016) suggested that besides the cost benefits, the value creation aspect of cloud computing should also be emphasized in research and practice. Ullrich, Cropper, Frühwirt, and Weippl (2016) suggested that in light of these changing paradigms with cloud computing, it is of utter importance to reconsider security.

The findings of the research were consistent with and aligned to Christensen's (1997) disruptive innovation theory, as it pertains to the usefulness of technological innovations in the evaluation process of adoption of cloud computing in an organization (Christensen, 2011; Crockett et al., 2013). All themes that emerged play a critical role in understanding this process, and the strategies that make it successful. This research thus contributes to understanding the strategies IT leaders use to adopt cloud computing.

The findings of the research were also consistent with the existing literature on effective business practices, including security strategies (Sobragi et al., 2014; Young Bae et al., 2013), competitive strategy (Dadameah & Costello, 2011; Liu et al., 2015), exit strategy (Schaffer, 2014), and business innovation strategy (Helland, 2013; Hu et al., 2013). According to Carcary, Doherty, and Conway (2014), IT leaders should completely understand the importance of adoption of cloud computing. Sobragi et al. (2014) also suggested that cloud computing's adoption will increase as some of the user adoption concerns, including security, performance, and interoperability, are addressed. Therefore, understanding strategies to adopt cloud computing is as important for the end users as it is for IT leaders. When there are no strategies in place to adopt cloud computing, IT leaders may have a greater challenge in doing so, and in maintaining profitability and sustainability.

Applications to Professional Practice

Strategies to adopt cloud computing benefit the professional practices by: (a) adding to business agility, (b) creating new business models, (c) reducing operational issues, (d) improving utilization of resources, and (e) reducing capital expense requirements to support application and IT infrastructure (Alshamaila, Papagiannidis, & Li, 2013; Park & Kim, 2014; Trigueros-Preciado et al., 2013). However, the slow adoption of cloud computing has been an increasing concern for IT leaders (Sobragi et al., 2014).

Services offered by cloud computing are ideal for businesses with growing or fluctuating bandwidth demands (Alshamaila et al., 2013). If the company needs to grow, leaders should find it easy to scale-up the cloud computing infrastructure capacity, leveraging the remote standby servers in the cloud computing environment (Alshamaila et al., 2013). Similarly, if the IT leaders need to scale down again, they can, by leveraging cloud computing service (Park & Kim, 2014).

IT leaders may enhance business value when making major choices about IT infrastructure by leveraging cloud computing adoption strategies (Park & Kim, 2014). Almost all participants in my research mentioned that using cloud computing can reduce the dependence on the traditional IT staff. As such, IT leaders can start using the cloud services on a smaller scale with non-mission critical workloads to evaluate the cloud services offerings by different cloud services providers.

The increased nimbleness offered by cloud computing helps businesses with quick time-to-market and, as a result, to appeal to new consumers promptly (Mohlameane & Ruxwana, 2014; Trigueros-Preciado et al., 2013). The reduced time-to-market not only attracts new customers who otherwise would have gone to competitors but also averts those competitors from taking away market share (Katzan, 2010). Therefore, adoption of cloud computing improves the company's competitive strength in the marketplace (Liu et al., 2015). Participants in my study explicitly stated that the time-to-market for their application development cycles significantly improved with cloud computing services.

An additional point of interest is the fact that IT organizational spendings are shifting from CapEx (Capital Expenditures) to OpEx (Operational Expenditures) models (Nanath & Pillai, 2013). IT leaders do not have to buy IT assets any longer, but instead, rent or lease them from cloud computing service providers and consume them in a utility model as long as the customers need them (Andersen et al., 2013; Nanath & Pillai, 2013). Once customers do not require the IT service anymore, IT leaders discontinue the usage of the service with the cloud service provider to optimize costs (Nanath & Pillai, 2013). All participants in my study mentioned that by leveraging the strategies to adopt cloud computing, they lowered the total costs transition from a fixed cost structure to a variable one while making valuable IT resources available for strategic initiatives and innovation.

Time to value with cloud computing solutions is considerably lower than with on-premise applications (Bala Subrahmanya, 2013; Henard & McFadyen, 2012). Cloud computing solutions may reduce the time to value from 2 to 3 years to 2 to 3 quarters (Katzan, 2010). Cloud computing solutions reduce implementation time as well as the IT resources required to roll-out the solution (Trigueros-Preciado et al., 2013). All participants in my research mentioned that the time to value with cloud computing solutions was significantly lower than the traditional on-premise application. Also, with an appropriately defined exit strategy, cloud solutions provide an easy out if the customer is dissatisfied with the cloud computing services offering, therefore transferring the risk from the consumer of cloud services to the cloud computing service provider (Dahl, 2011; Henard & McFadyen, 2012; Schaffer, 2014).

Finally, mobility is increasingly critical since small- to medium-sized companies are scattered around the world; access from anywhere is crucial for the success of any small to medium-sized company (Benedict, 2013; Sultan, 2014). All participants in my research mentioned that data mobility was one of the main elements in their cloud computing adoption strategies to improve their business practices. As IT leaders understand these strategies, the findings of the literature and primary research presented in this book may assist IT leaders in developing effective strategies to adopt cloud computing for their organization.

Recommendations for Practice

IT leaders may consider assessing their strategies against the findings presented in this book, which highlight the essential elements and effective strategies to adopt cloud computing. IT leaders need to start pursuing effective strategies to adopt cloud computing to sustain productivity, growth, and competitive advantage (Mohlameane & Ruxwana, 2014). If strategies do not exist within the organization, IT leaders should create such strategies and evaluate their efficacy in their organizational context. IT leaders should also evaluate the financial plans and budgets to allocated funding to support cloud computing adoption strategies. Overall, IT leaders must align their strategies with the corporate business objectives of their organizations. Thus, this book is valuable to researchers, company owners, IT leaders, and IT services consumers, for the application of effective cloud computing adoption strategies may enable IT leaders to use tangible procedures to strategize effectively to adopt cloud computing and sustain productivity for their organization.

Recommendations for Scholarship

The results of the primary research presented in this book warrant further exploration of strategies that IT leaders use to adopt cloud computing for their organization to sustain productivity, growth, and competitive advantage (Nanavati et al., 2014). Following are my recommendations for further research:

1. Examine cloud computing adoption strategies needed from the view of consumers of IT services, and not just those in IT leadership positions.

2. Explore the necessity for and impact of the strategies that IT leaders use to adopt cloud computing within and across different geographical locations.
3. Research strategies to adopt cloud computing with larger sample sizes or larger organizations.
4. Conduct a study to compare the strategies that IT leaders use to adopt cloud computing in for-profit versus non-profit organizations. A comparison between for-profit and non-profit business types may expose cloud computing adoption strategies most appropriate for the budget allocations and operations for each business classification.
5. Identify the factors in measuring the effectiveness of different cloud computing adoption strategies.
6. Finally, assess the effect of cloud computing adoption strategies on an organization's productivity and viability.

Final Thoughts

In addition to its business and theoretical implications, innovations like cloud computing hold implications for social change and benefits for the community writ large. For example, it holds the potential to upsurge the productivity of businesses and improve economies (Carcary et al., 2014; Song et al., 2013). Growth in business productivity makes businesses viable and enables business leaders to make positive offerings to society by enhancing the fortune of stockholders, creating employment opportunities, and contributing to the government's tax proceeds (Moyano, Fernandez-Gago, & Lopez, 2013). Without the exorbitant costs involved in the creation and management of IT infrastructures, critical services and IT leaders and business owners can now get speedy access to the IT support, applications, and data storage they need (Song et al., 2013). The prompt availability of IT resources provided by cloud computing services enables IT leaders to develop, progress, and offer superior services to their customers (Moyano et al., 2013). The superior services in turn benefit and help build a strong economy. The adoption of cloud computing also reduces hardware requirements in developing countries and supports developing economies (Dadameah & Costello, 2011; Trigueros-Preciado et al., 2013).

The data further showed that "cloud computing has a direct and indirect positive impact on our environment" (Participant 2). Adopting cloud computing may provide air conditioning and electricity, and reduce the power and cooling requirements of datacenters (Alshamaila et al., 2013), as well as decrease greenhouse gas emissions (Trigueros-Preciado et al., 2013).

Finally, the adoption of cloud computing may also influence how we communicate, how and where we can access information, and how the news is reported, as well as access to services (Dadameah & Costello, 2011). Adoption of cloud computing-based communication has opened up communication between friends and family who may live thousands of miles away but want to keep in contact frequently (Carcary et al., 2014). This resource sharing and communication makes it simpler to share information swiftly and securely (Katzan, 2010). This capability further holds benefits for public services such as education, healthcare, and law enforcement (Carcary et al., 2014; Song et al., 2013).

It is for these reasons that cloud computing offers IT leaders—and business organizations more generally—a powerful, innovative, and beneficial tool to decrease costs and increase their competitive advantage, profits, and outcomes. With the knowledge and findings presented in this book, IT leaders now have the resource needed to adopt cloud computing successfully in their organization.

References

Abouelhoda, M., Issa, S. A., & Ghanem, M. (2012). Tavaxy: Integrating taverna and galaxy workflows with cloud computing support. *BMC Bioinformatics, 13*, 1-19. doi:10.1186/1471-2105-13-77

Alali, F. A., & Yeh, C. L. (2012). Cloud computing: Overview and risk analysis. *Journal of Information Systems, 26*(2), 13-33. doi:10.2308/isys-50229

Aleem, A., & Christopher, R. S. (2013). Let me in the cloud: Analysis of the benefit and risk assessment of cloud platform. *Journal of Financial Crime, 20*, 6-24. doi:10.1108/13590791311287337

Ali, A. M., & Yusof, H. (2011). Quality in qualitative studies: The case of validity, reliability, and generalizability. *Issue in Social & Environmental Accounting, 5*(1), 25-64. Retrieved from http://www.iiste.org/Journals/index.php/ISEA/index

Alshamaila, Y., Papagiannidis, S., & Li, F. (2013). Cloud computing adoption by SMEs in the north east of England. *Journal of Enterprise Information Management, 26*, 250-275. doi:10.1108/17410391311325225

Andersen, S., Gupta, M., & Gupta, A. (2013). A managerial decision-making web app: Goldratt's evaporating cloud. *International Journal of Production Research, 51*, 2505-2517. doi:10.1080/00207543.2012.743687

Andrikopoulos, V., Binz, T., Leymann, F., & Strauch, S. (2013). How to adapt applications for the cloud environment. *Computing: Archives for Informatics and Numerical Computation, 95*, 493-535. doi:10.1007/s00607-012-0248-2

Aoyama, T., & Sakai, H. (2011). *Business & Information Systems Engineering, 3*, 172-177.

Arora, A., & Nandkumar, A. (2012). Insecure advantage? Markets for technology and the value of resources for entrepreneurial ventures. *Strategic Management Journal, 33*, 231-251. doi:10.1002/smj.953

Bala Subrahmanya, M. H. (2013). External support, innovation, and economic performance: What firm level factors matter for high-tech SMEs? How? *International Journal of Innovation Management, 17*(5), 1-26. doi:10.1142/S1363919613500242

Bao Rong, C., Hsiu-Fen, T., & Chi-Ming, C. (2013). Empirical analysis of server consolidation and desktop virtualization in cloud computing. *Mathematical Problems in Engineering*, 1-11. doi:10.1155/2013/947234

Barratt, M., Choi, T. Y., & Li, M. (2011). Qualitative case studies in operations management: Trends, research outcomes, and future research implications. *Journal of Operations Management, 29*, 329-342. doi:10.1016/j.jom.2010.06.002

Barrett, E., Howley, E., & Duggan, J. (2013). Applying reinforcement learning towards automating resource allocation and application scalability in the cloud. *Concurrency & Computation: Practice &*

Experience, 25, 1656-1674.
doi:10.1002/cpe.2864

Benedict, S. (2013). Performance issues and
performance analysis tools for HPC cloud
applications: A survey. *Computing:
Archives for Informatics and Numerical
Computation, 95*, 89-108.
doi:10.1007/s00607-012-0213-0

Budrienė, D., & Zalieckaitė, L. (2012). Cloud
computing application in small and med-
sized enterprises. *Issues of Business & Law,
4*, 199-130. doi:10.520/ibl.2012.11

Bugnion, E., Devine, S., Rosenblum, M., Sugerman,
J., & Wang, E. Y. (2012). Bringing
virtualization to the x86 architecture with
the original VMware workstation. *ACM
Transactions on Computer Systems, 50*(4),
1-51. doi:10.1145/2382553.2382554

Business models for strategy and innovation.
(2012). *Communications of the ACM, 55*(7),
22-24. doi:10.1145/2209249.2209259

Cambra-Fierro, J., & Wilson, A. (2011). Qualitative
data analysis software: Will it ever become
mainstream? *International Journal of
Market Research, 53*(1), 17-24. Retrieved
from http://www.ijmr.com/

Carcary, M., Doherty, E., & Conway, G. (2014).
The adoption of cloud computing by Irish
SMEs: An exploratory study. *Electronic
Journal of Information Systems Evaluation,
17*(1), 3-14. Retrieved from
http://www.ejise.com/main.html

Cavage, M. (2013). There is no getting around it:
You are building a distributed system.

Communications of the ACM, 56(6), 63-70.
doi:10.1145/2461256.2461274

Caytiles, D. R., & Lee, S. (2012). Security
considerations for public mobile cloud
computing. *International Journal of
Advanced Science and Technology, 44*, 81-
88. Retrieved from
http://www.sersc.org/journals/IJAST/

Chandrashekhar, A. M., Gupta, R. K., & Shivaraj,
H. P. (2015). Role of information security
awareness in success of an organization.
International Journal of Research, 2(6), 15-
22. Retrieved from
http://internationaljournalofresearch.org/

Chang, V., Walters, R. J., & Wills, G. (2013). The
development that leads to the cloud
computing business framework.
*International Journal of Information
Management, 33*, 524-538.
doi:10.1016/j.ijinfomgt.2013.01.005

Changsoo, L., Daewon, J., & Keunwang, L. (2013).
Survey on security threats and security
technology analysis for secured cloud
services. *International Journal of Security &
Its Applications, 7*(6), 21-29.
doi:10.14257/ijsia.2013.7.6.03

Chao, L. (2014). Design of cloud services for cloud
based IT education. *Journal of Information
Technology and Application in Education, 3*,
106-112. doi:10.14355
/jitae.2014.0303.03

Chauhan, M., Malhotra, R., Pathak, M., & Singh, U.
P. (2012). Different aspects of cloud
security. *International Journal of
Engineering Research and Applications, 2*,

864-869. Retrieved from
http://www.ijera.com

Choudhary, V., & Vithayathil, J. (2013). The
impact of cloud computing: Should the IT
department be organized as a cost center or a
profit center? *Journal of Management
Information Systems, 30*(2), 67-100.
doi:10.2753/MIS0742-1222300203

Christensen, C. (1997). *The innovator's dilemma.*
New York, NY: Harper Business Essentials.

Christensen, C. M. (2011). *The innovator's
dilemma: The revolutionary book that will
change the way you do business.* New York,
NY: Harper Business Essentials.

Clarke, R. (2012). How reliable is cloudsourcing? A
review of articles in the technical media
2005-11. *Computer Law & Security Review,
28*, 90-95. doi:10.1016/j.clsr.2011.11.010

Cohen, J. E. (2013). What privacy is for? *Harvard
Law Review, 126*, 1904-1933. Retrieved
from http://www.cdn.harvardlawreview.org

Crockett, D. R., McGee, J. E., & Payne, G. T.
(2013). Employing new business divisions
to exploit disruptive innovations: The
interplay between characteristics of the
corporation and those of the venture
management team. *Journal of Product
Innovation Management, 30*, 856-879.
doi:10.1111/jpim.12034

Dadameah, S. M., & Costello, P. (2011). A study on
higher education institutions' influence
towards competitive strategy development in
an ICT cluster. *Journal of Organizational
Transformation & Social Change, 8*, 123-
142. doi:10.1386/jots.8.2.123_1

Dahl, D. W. (2011). Clarity in defining product design: Inspiring research opportunities for the design process. *Journal of Product Innovation Management, 28*, 425-427. doi:10.1111/j.1540-5885.2011.00816.x

Dan, Y., & Chang Chieh, H. (2010). A reflective review of disruptive innovation theory. *International Journal of Management Reviews, 12*, 435-452. doi:10.1111/j.1468-2370.2009.00272.x

DaSilva, C. M., Trkman, P., Desouza, K., & Lindič, J. (2013). Disruptive technologies: A business model perspective on cloud computing. *Technology Analysis & Strategic Management, 25*, 1161-1173. doi:10.1080/09537325.2013.843661

Demirkan, H., & Dolk, D. (2013). Analytical, computational, and conceptual modeling in service science and systems. *Information Systems & e-Business Management, 11*, 1-11. doi:10.1007/s10257-012-0189-5

Desai, D. (2013). Beyond location: Data security in the 21st century. *Communications of the ACM, 56*(1), 34-36. doi:10.1145/2398356.2398368

Faniyi, F., & Bahsoon, R. (2016). A systematic review of service level management in the cloud. *ACM Computing Surveys, 48*(3), 1-43. doi:10.1145/2843890

Fernando, N., Loke, S. W., & Rahayu, W. (2013). Mobile cloud computing: A survey. *Future Generation Computer Systems, 29*, 84-106. doi:10.1016/j.future.2012.05.023

Flores, W. R., Antonsen, E., & Ekstedt, M. (2014). Information security knowledge sharing in organizations: Investigating the effect of behavioral information security governance and national culture. *Computers & Security, 43*, 90-110. doi:10.1016/j.cose.2014.03.004

Franzosi, R., Doyle, S., McClelland, L., Putnam Rankin, C., & Vicari, S. (2013). Quantitative narrative analysis software options compared: PC-ACE and CAQDAS (ATLAS.ti, MAXqda, and NVivo). *Quality & Quantity, 47*, 3219-3247. doi:10.1007/s11135-012-9714-3

Frey, S., Hasselbring, W., & Schnoor, B. (2013). Automatic conformance checking for migrating software systems to cloud infrastructures and platforms. *Journal of Software: Evolution & Process, 25*, 1089-1115. doi:10.1002/smr.582

García, A., Espert, I., & García, V. (2014). SLA-driven dynamic cloud resource management. *Future Generation Computer Systems, 31*, 1-11. doi:10.1016/j .future.2013.10.005

Garg, S. K., Versteeg, S., & Buyya, R. (2013). A framework for ranking of cloud computing services. *Future Generation Computer Systems, 29*, 1012-1023. doi:10.1016/j.future.2012.06.006

Garrison, G., Kim, S., & Wakefield, R. L. (2012). Success factors for deploying cloud computing. *Communications of the ACM, 55*(9), 62-68. doi:10.1145/2330667.2330685

Gibson, J., & Kasravi, K. (2012). Predicting the future of IT services with TRIZ. *Journal of Integrated Design & Process Science, 16*, 5-14. Retrieved from http://www.dl.acm.org

Giessmann, A., & Stanoevska-Slabeva, K. (2012). Business models of platform as a service (PaaS) providers: Current state and future directions. *Journal of Information Technology Theory and Application, 13*(4), 31-54. Retrieved from http://www.aisel.aisnet.org

Gold, J. (2012). Protection in the cloud: Risk management and insurance for cloud computing. *Journal of Internet Law, 15*(12), 1-28. Retrieved from http://www.aspenpublishers.com

Goutas, L., Sutanto, J., & Aldarbesti, H. (2016). The building blocks of a cloud strategy: Evidence from three SaaS providers. *Communications of the ACM, 59*(1), 90-97. doi:10.1145/2756545

Haimes, Y. Y., & Chittister, C. C. (2012). Risk to cyber infrastructure systems served by cloud computing technology as systems of systems. *Systems Engineering, 15*, 213-224. doi:10.1002/sys.20204

Heale, R., & Forbes, D. (2013). Understanding triangulation in research. *Evid Based Nurs, 16*, 98. doi:10.1136/eb-2013-101494

Helland, P. (2013). Condos and clouds. *Communications of the ACM, 56*(1), 50-59. doi:10.1145/2398356.2398374

Henard, D. H., & McFadyen, M. (2012). Resource dedication and new product performance: A resource-based view. *Journal of Product Innovation Management, 29*, 193-204. doi:10.1111/j.1540-5885.2011.00889.x

Heng, Z., Fu, Y., Liu, G., Zhou, R., Wang, Y., Yuan, R., & Dong, X. (2014). A study of the distribution and variability of cloud water using ISCCP, SSM/I cloud product, and reanalysis datasets. *Journal of Climate, 27,* 3114-3128. doi:10.1175/JCLI-D-13-00031.1

Hu, J., Deng, J., & Wu, J. (2013). A green private cloud architecture with global collaboration. *Telecommunication Systems, 52,* 1269-1279. doi:10.1007/s11235-011-9639-5

Huang, C. Y., Chen, K. T., Chen, D. Y., Hsu, H. J., & Hsu, C. H. (2014). GamingAnywhere: The first open source cloud gaming system. *ACM Transactions on Multimedia Computing, Communications & Applications, 10*(2), 1-25. doi:10.1145/2537855

Huang, S., Wu, M., & Chen, L. (2013). Critical success factors in aligning IT and business objectives: A Delphi study. *Total Quality Management & Business Excellence, 24,* 1219-1240. doi:10.1080/14783363.2011.637785

Hyman, P. (2013). Augmented-reality glasses bring cloud security into sharp focus. *Communications of the ACM, 56*(6), 18-20. doi:10.1145/2461256.2461264

Iyer, B., & Henderson, J. C. (2012). Business value from clouds: Learning from users. *MIS Quarterly Executive, 11*(1), 51-60. Retrieved from http://www.misqe.samicspa.com

Jabbari Sabegh, M., & Motlagh, S. (2012). The role and relevance of IT governance and IT capability in business: IT alignment in medium and large companies. *Business & Management Review, 2*(6), 16-23. Retrieved from http://www.businessjournalz.org

Jamsa, K. (2013). *Cloud computing: SaaS, PaaS, IaaS, virtualization, business models, mobile, security and more.* Jones & Bartlett Learning.

Jeon, H., Min, Y. G., & Seo, K. K. (2014). A framework of performance measurement monitoring of cloud service infrastructure system for service activation. *International Journal of Software Engineering & its Applications, 8*(5), 127-138. Retrieved from http://www.sersc.org/journals/IJSEIA/

Jing, S., Ali, S., She, K., & Zhong, Y. (2013). State-of-the-art research study for green cloud computing. *Journal of Supercomputing, 65,* 445-468. doi:10.1007/s11227-011-0722-1

Juels, A., & Oprea, A. (2013). New approaches to security and availability for cloud data. *Communications of the ACM, 56*(2), 64-73. doi:10.1145/2408776.2408793

Karadsheh, L. (2012). Applying security policies and service level agreement to IaaS service model to enhance security and transition. *Computers & Security, 31,* 315-326. doi:10.1016/j.cose.2012.01.003

Katzan, H., Jr. (2010). The education value of cloud computing. *Contemporary Issues in Education Research, 3*(7), 37-42. Retrieved from http://www.royastleyfryer.com

Kaur, T., & Chana, I. (2015). Energy efficiency techniques in cloud computing: A survey and taxonomy. *ACM Computing Surveys, 48*(2), 1-22. doi:10.1145/2742488

Kipkulei, K. (2013). Effects of information technology on reducing perishable waste in supermarkets. *Dissertation Abstracts*

International: Section B: Sciences and Engineering, 74/08(E). (UMI No. 3560427)

Kuang-Hua, H., Fu-Hsiang, C., & Wei-Jhou, W. (2016). Exploring the key risk factors for application of cloud computing in auditing. *Entropy, 18*(8), 1-24. doi:10.3390/e18080401

Kumar, A., & Sharma, Y. K. (2017). A hybrid optimized framework for cloud resource management system. *International Journal of Recent Research Aspects, 4*(3), 31-33.

Kumthekar, N., & Aserkar, R. (2012). Study of current software trends of logistics service providers with feasibility of cloud computing as an alternative. *Skyline Business Journal, 7*(1), 41-50. Retrieved from http://www.skylineuniversity.com

Kun, H., Ming, X., Shaojing, F., & Jian, L. (2014). Securing the cloud storage audit service: Defending against frame and collude attacks of third party auditor. *IET Communications, 8*, 2106-2113. doi:10.1049/iet-com.2013.0898

Lacity, M. C., & Reynolds, P. (2014). Cloud services practices for small and medium-sized enterprises. *MIS Quarterly Executive, 13*(1), 31-44. Retrieved from http://www.misqe.samicspa.com

Lai, K., & Yu, Y. (2012). A scalable multi-attribute hybrid overlay for range queries on the cloud. *Information Systems Frontiers, 14*, 895-908. doi:10.1007/s10796-011-9328-7

Lal, P., & Bharadwaj, S. S. (2015). Assessing the performance of cloud-based customer relationship management systems. *Skyline*

Business Journal, 11(1), 89-100. Retrieved from http://www.skylineuniversity.com

Lango, J. (2014). Toward software- Defined SLAs. *Communications of the ACM, 57*(1), 54-60. doi:10.1145/2541883.2541894

Li, C., & Li, L. (2013). Efficient resource allocation for optimizing objectives of cloud users, IaaS provider and SaaS provider in cloud environment. *Journal of Supercomputing, 65*, 866-885. doi:10.1007/s11227-013-0869-z

Li, J., Zhao, G., Rong, C., & Tang, Y. (2013). Semantic description of scholar-oriented social network cloud. *Journal of Supercomputing, 65*, 410-425. doi:10.1007/s11227-010-0550-8

Li, S., Xu, L., Wang, X., & Wang, J. (2012). Integration of hybrid wireless networks in cloud services oriented enterprise information systems. *Enterprise Information Systems, 6*(2), 165-187. doi:10.1080/17517575.2011.654266

Lin, B., Hsiao, P., Cheng, P., Lee, I., & Jan, G. E. (2015). Design and implementation of a set-top box-based homecare system using hybrid cloud. *Telemedicine & E-Health, 21*(11), 916-922. doi:10.1089/tmj.2014.0244

Lin, Y., & Chang, P. (2013). Performance indicator evaluation for a cloud computing system from QoS viewpoint. *Quality and Quantity, 47*, 1605-1616. doi:10.1007 /s11135-011-613-z

Litke, A. et al. (2007). Consolidated report on the implementation of the infrastructure services layer version 1.0. *Akogrimo Consortium.*

Retrieved from
http://www.akogrimo.org/modulesa3f9.pdf

Liu, S., Yang, Y., Qu, W. G., & Liu, Y. (2016). The
business value of cloud computing: The
partnering agility perspective. *Industrial
Management & Data Systems, 116*(6), 1160-
1177. doi:10.1108/imds-09-2015-0376

Liu, Y., Sheng, X., & Marston, S. R. (2015). The
impact of client-side security restrictions on
the competition of cloud computing
services. *International Journal of Electronic
Commerce, 19*(3), 90-117.
doi:10.1080/10864415.2015.1000224

Madhani, P. (2012). Marketing and supply chain
management integration: A resource-based
view of competitive advantages.
*International Journal of Value Chain
Management, 6*, 216-239.
doi:10.1504/IJVCM.2012.050863

Manias, E., & Baude, F. (2012). A component-
based middleware for hybrid grid/cloud
computing platforms. *Concurrency &
Computation: Practice & Experience, 24*,
1461-1477. doi:10.1002/cpe.2822

Mauch, V., Kunze, M., & Hillenbrand, M. (2012).
High performance cloud computing. *Future
Generation Computer Systems, 29*, 1408-
1416. doi:10.1016/j.future.2012.03.011

Maxwell, J. A. (2013). *Qualitative research design:
An interactive approach* (3rd ed.). Thousand
Oaks, CA: Sage.

Mazhelis, O., & Tyrväinen, P. (2012). Economic
aspects of hybrid cloud infrastructure: User
organization perspective. *Information*

Systems Frontiers, 14, 845-869.
doi:10.1007/s10796-011-9326-9

McMurtry, J. (2012). Behind global system
collapse: The life-blind structure of
economic rationality. *Journal of Business
Ethics, 108*, 49-60. doi:10.1007/s10551-011-086-4

Mehraeen, E., Ghazisaeedi, M., Farzi, J., &
Mirshekari, S. (2017). Security Challenges
in Healthcare Cloud Computing: A
Systematic Review. *International Journal of
Engineering Research and Technology, 9*(3),
511–517. Retrieved from
https://www.ijert.org/

Mladenow, A., Kryvinska, N., & Strauss, C. (2012).
Towards cloud-centric service
environments. *Journal of Service Science
Research, 4*, 213-234. doi:10.1007/s12927-012-0009-y

Mohlameane, M., & Ruxwana, N. (2014). The
awareness of cloud computing: A case study
of South African SMEs. *International
Journal of Trade, Economics, and Finance,
5*, 6-11. doi:10.7763IJTEF.2014.V5.332

Morse, A., & McEvoy, C. D. (2014). Qualitative
research in sport management: Case study as
a methodological approach. *The Qualitative
Report, 19*(31), 1-13. Retrieved from
http://nsuworks.nova.edu/tqr

Moyano, F., Fernandez-Gago, C., & Lopez, J.
(2013). A framework for enabling trust
requirements in social cloud applications.
Requirements Engineering, 18, 321-341.
doi:10.1007/s00766-013-0171-x

Nadjaran Toosi, A., Calheiros, R. N., & Buyya, R. (2014). Interconnected cloud computing environments: Challenges, taxonomy, and survey. *ACM Computing Surveys, 47*(1), Art. 7. doi:10.1145/2593512

Nallur, V., & Bahsoon, R. (2013). A decentralized self-adaptation mechanism for service-based applications in the cloud. *IEEE Transactions on Software Engineering, 39*, 591-612. doi:10.1109/TSE.2012.53

Nanath, K., & Pillai, R. (2013). A model for cost-benefit analysis of cloud computing. *Journal of International Technology and Information Management, 22*(3), 95-110. Retrieved from http://www.iima.org

Nanavati, M., Colp, P., Aiello, B., & Warfield, A. (2014). Cloud security: A gathering storm. *Communications of the ACM, 57*(5), 70-79. doi:10.1145/2593686

Narayanan, V. (2012). Harnessing the cloud: International law implications of cloud-computing. *Chicago Journal of International Law, 12*, 783-809. Retrieved from http://wwwcjil.uchicago.edu/

Nassim Aryani, N. (2014). IT and agility features at the organization (A case study). *International Journal of Academic Research, 6*, 268-273. doi:10.7813/2075-4124.2014/6-1/A.35

Neumann, P. G. (2014). Risks and myths of cloud computing and cloud storage. *Communications of the ACM, 57*(10), 25-27. doi:10.1145/2661049

Nevala, H., Ollila-Tåg, C., Pitkäkoski, P., Takala, J., & Toivola, J. (2012). A research of critical factors in the cloud service approach. *Management, 7*(1), 73-83. Retrieved from http://www.fm-kp.si/zalozba/ISSN/1854-4231.htm

Oliveros, E., Cucinotta, T., Phillips, S. C., Yang, X., Middleton, S., & Voith, T. (2012). Monitoring and metering in the cloud. In *Achieving real-time in distributed computing: From grids to clouds* (pp. 94-114). IGI Global.

Onsongo, G., Erdmann, J., Spears, M. D., Chilton, J., Beckman, K. B., Hauge, A., & Thyagarajan, B. (2014). Implementation of cloud based next generation sequencing data analysis in a clinical laboratory. *BMC Research Notes, 7*(1), 1-14. doi:10.1186/1756-0500-7-314

Park, E., & Kim, K. J. (2014). An integrated adoption model of mobile cloud services: Exploration of key determinants and extension of technology acceptance model. *Telematics and Informatics, 31*, 376-385. doi:10.1016/j.tele.2013.11.008

Pearce, M., Zeadally, S., & Hunt, R. (2013). Virtualization: Issues, security threats, and solutions. *ACM Computing Surveys, 45*(2), 17-39. doi:10.1145/2431211.2431216

Pedersen, T., Pedersen, D., & Riis, K. (2013). On-demand multidimensional data integration: Toward a semantic foundation for cloud intelligence. *Journal of Supercomputing, 65*, 217-257. doi:10.1007/s11227-011-0712-3

Petty, N., Thomson, O., & Stewa, G. (2012). Ready for a paradigm shift? Part 2: Introducing qualitative research methodologies and methods. *Manual Therapy, 17,* 378-384. doi:10.1016/j.math.2012.03.004

Poulymenopoulou, M., Malamateniou, F., & Vassilacopoulos, G. (2012). Emergency healthcare process automation using mobile computing and cloud services. *Journal of Medical Systems, 36,* 3233-3241. doi:10.1007/s10916-011-9814-y

Priem, R. L., & Swink, M. (2012). A demand-side perspective on supply chain management. *Journal of Supply Chain Management, 48,* 7-13. doi:10.1111/j.1745-493X.2012.03264.x

Rahman, N. H. B., & Choo, K. K. R. (2015). A survey of information security incident handling in the cloud. *Computers & Security, 49,* 45-69. doi:10.1016/j.cose.2014.11.006

Ralyté, J., Khadraoui, A., & Léonard, M. (2015). Designing the shift from information systems to information services systems. *Business & Information Systems Engineering, 57*(1), 37-49.

Roberts, N., & Grover, V. (2012). Leveraging information technology infrastructure to facilitate a firm's customer agility and competitive activity: An empirical investigation. *Journal of Management Information Systems, 28*(4), 231-270. doi:10.2753/mis0742-1222280409

Russel, S., & Millar, H. (2014). Exploring the relationships among sustainable manufacturing practices, business performance and competitive advantage: Perspectives from a developing economy.

Journal of Management and Sustainability,
4, 37-53. doi:10.5539/jms.v4n3p37

Sakhuja, D. U., & Shukla, A. (2013). Cloud
computing. *International Journal of
Engineering & Technology, 2*(3), 1-7.
Retrieved from http://www.ijert.org

Sanghyun, J. (2014). Study on service models of
digital textbooks in cloud computing
environment for SMART education.
*International Journal of U- & E-Service,
Science & Technology, 7*(1), 73-82.
Retrieved from
http://www.sersc.org/journals /IJUNESST/

Schaffer, H. (2014). Will you ever need an exit
strategy? *IT Professional, 16*(2), 4-6.
doi:10.1109/MITP.2014.25

Schweitzer, E. J. (2012). Reconciliation of the cloud
computing model with U.S. federal
electronic health record regulations. *Journal
of the American Medical Informatics
Association, 19*, 161-165.
doi:10.1136/amiajnl-2011-000162

Shinder, T. (2013). Hybrid cloud infrastructure
design considerations - TechNet articles -
United States (English) - TechNet wiki.
Retrieved from
https://social.technet.microsoft.com/wiki/co
ntents/articles/18120.hybrid-cloud-
infrastructure-design-
considerations.aspx#Hybrid_IT_Problem_D
efinition

Sindhu, R., & Mushtaque, M. (2014). A new
innovation on user's level security for
storage data in cloud computing.
International Journal of Grid & Distributed

Computing, 7, 213-219.
doi:10.14257/ijgdc.2014.7.3.22

Sinkovics, R., & Alfoldi, E. (2012). Progressive
focusing and trustworthiness in qualitative
research. *Management International Review,
52*, 817-845. doi:10.1007/s11575-012-0140-
5

Sobragi, C. G., Gastaud Macada, A. C., & Oliveira,
M. (2014). Cloud computing adoption: A
multiple case study. *Base, 11*, 75-91.
doi:10.4013/base.2014.111.06

Song, J., Li, T., Wang, Z., & Zhu, Z. (2013). Study
on energy-consumption regularities of cloud
computing systems by a novel evaluation
model. *Computing: Archives for Informatics
and Numerical Computation, 95*, 269-287.
doi:10.1007/s00607-012-0218-8

Srinivasan, S. S. (2013). Is security realistic in
cloud computing? *Journal of International
Technology & Information Management,
22*(4), 47-66. Retrieved from
http://www.iima.org/

Srivastava, H., & Kumar, S. A. (2015). Control
framework for secure cloud computing.
Journal of Information Security, 6, 12-23.
doi:10.4236/jis.2015.61002

Sultan, N. (2014). Making use of cloud computing
for healthcare provision: Opportunities and
challenges. *International Journal of
Information Management, 34*, 177-184.
doi:10.1016/j.ijinfomgt.2013.12.011

Sultan, N., & van de Bunt-Kokhuis, S. (2012).
Organizational culture and cloud computing:
Coping with a disruptive innovation.
Technology Analysis & Strategic

Management, *24*, 167-179.
doi:10.1080/09537325.2012.647644

Sunyaev, A., & Schneider, S. (2013). Cloud
services certification. *Communications of
the ACM, 56*(2), 33-36.
doi:10.1145/2408776.2408789

Tan, C., & Teh, Y. (2013). Synthetic hardware
performance analysis in virtualized cloud
environment for healthcare organization.
Journal of Medical Systems, 37(4), 1-13.
doi:10.1007/s10916-013-9950-7

Thanakornworakij, T., Nassar, R., Leangsuksun, C.,
& Paun, M. (2013). A reliability model for
cloud computing for high performance
computing applications, Euro-Par 2012:
Parallel processing workshops. *Lecture
Notes in Computer Science Volume, 7640*,
474-483. doi:10.1007/978-3-642-36949-
0_53

Trigueros-Preciado, S., Pérez-González, D., &
Solana-González, P. (2013). Cloud
computing in industrial SMEs: Identification
of the barriers to its adoption and effects of
its application. *Electronic Markets, 23*, 105-
114. doi:10.1007/s12525-012-0120-4

Uchechukwu, A., Li, K., & Shen, Y. (2012).
Improving cloud computing energy
efficiency. *2012 IEEE Asia Pacific Cloud
Computing Congress.*
doi:10.1109/apcloudcc.2012.6486511

Ullrich, J., Cropper, J., Frühwirt, P., & Weippl, E.
(2016). The role and security of firewalls in
cyber-physical cloud computing. *EURASIP
Journal on Information Security, 2016*(1), 1-
20. doi:10.1186/s13635-016-0042-3

Ussahawanitchakit, P. (2012). Information richness, marketing effectiveness, IT comprtency, and competitive advantage: Evidence from Thai e-commerce businesses. *Journal of International Business Strategy, 12*(1), 10-18. Retrieved from http://www.iabe.org

Walterbusch, M., Martens, B., & Teuteberg, F. (2013). Evaluating cloud computing services from a total cost of ownership perspective. *Management Research Review, 36*, 613-638. doi:10.1108/01409171311325769

Wang, L., & Alexander, C. A. (2013). Medical applications and healthcare based on cloud computing. *International Journal of Cloud Computing and Services Science, 2*, 217-225. doi:10.11591/closer.v2i4.3452

Wenge, O., Lampe, U., Rensing, C., & Steinmetz, R. (2014). Security information and event monitoring as a service: A survey on current concerns and solutions. *Praxis Der Informationsverarbeitung und Kommunikation, 37*, 163-170. doi:10.1515/pik-2014-0009

Xiaolong, C., Mills, B., Znati, T., & Melhem, R. (2014). Shadow replication: An energy-aware, fault-tolerant computational model for green cloud computing. *Energies, 7*, 5151-5176. doi:10.3390/en7085151

Ye, N., Yang, S. S., & Aranda, B. M. (2013). The analysis of service provider-user coordination for resource allocation in cloud computing. *Information Knowledge Systems Management, 12*, 1-24. doi:10.3233/IKS-2002-00214

Yin, R. K. (2014). *Case study research design and methods* (5th ed.). Thousand Oaks, CA: Sage.

Yoo, S., Kim, S., Kim, T., Baek, R. M., Suh, C. S., Chung, C. Y., & Hwang, H. (2012). Economic analysis of cloud-based desktop virtualization implementation at a hospital. *BMC Medical Informatics & Decision Making, 12*, 119-124. doi:10.1186/1472-6947-12-119

Young Bae, Y., Junseok, O., & Bong Gyou, L. (2013). The establishment of security strategies for introducing cloud computing. *KSII Transactions on Internet & Information Systems, 7*, 860-877. doi:10.3837/tiis.2013.04.015

Zissis, D., & Lekkas, D. (2012). Addressing cloud computing security issues. *Future Generation Computer Systems, 28*, 583-592. doi:10.1016/j.future.2010.12.006

Glossary

Application-as-a-service (AaaS). The application-as-a-service cloud delivery model provides end users the capability to leverage a prebuilt application service catalog without deploying any underlying hardware and application software infrastructure (Karadsheh, 2012). An AaaS model includes prebuilt and pre-provisioned storage, network, computing, operating system, and application environment to support data processing (Karadsheh, 2012).

Cloud computing. Cloud computing is a method of computing over the Internet (Andersen et al., 2013). Cloud computing includes highly scalable information and technological competencies consumed as a service in a utility model (Andersen et al., 2013).

Cost centers. Cost centers are internal departments of an organization that do not influence profit directly but indirectly add to the cost of doing business (Mauch, Kunze, & Hillenbrand, 2012). Examples include marketing, IT, and research and development (Mauch et al., 2012).

Data centers. Data centers are facilities that host all technology and infrastructure resources, including software, computing, networking, and data storage resources (Mauch et al., 2012).

Infrastructure-as-a-service (IaaS). Infrastructure-as-a-service is a cloud computing delivery model that enables end users to leverage the core hardware components in a cloud-computing environment (Karadsheh, 2012). An IaaS model includes prebuilt and pre-provisioned storage, network, and computing environment ready for the operating system, application deployment, and data processing (Karadsheh, 2012).

Platform-as-a-service (PaaS). Platform-as-a-service is a cloud computing delivery model that enables end users to leverage the core hardware and essential software components in a cloud-computing environment (Karadsheh, 2012). A PaaS model includes prebuilt and pre-provisioned storage, network, computing, and operating system environment ready for application deployment and data processing (Karadsheh, 2012).

Software-as-a-service (SaaS). Software-as-a-service is a cloud computing delivery model that enables end users to deploy applications and functionality through remote access to web-based services or infrastructure on the Internet (Karadsheh, 2012). End users do not purchase software to install it on their workstations because cloud computing service providers own the software and license the use of the software to the end users (Karadsheh, 2012).

Virtualization. Virtualization allows for the consolidation of many physical data center resources into fewer physical resources that host various virtual and logical independent entities (Bao Rong, Hsiu-Fen, & Chi-Ming, 2013).

Author Biography

Dr. Zeeshan "Shawn" Khan is an Adjunct Assistant Professor at the University of Maryland University College, where he has developed several graduate courses for the Master's of Cloud Computing Architecture program. Dr. Khan is also a Technology Leader at a fortune 500 data management company, out of their New York office. In the past, Dr. Khan has held numerous technical leadership positions at small, mid-sized, and global organizations.

Dr. Khan lives in Long Island, NY with his wife and children. Dr. Khan has a Bachelor's degree in multidisciplinary studies (a combination of computer science, mathematics, and business courses) from Stony Brook University of State University of New York (SUNY), a Master's in business administration, and a Doctorate in business administration with a concentration in information systems management from Walden University Minneapolis, MN.

Dr. Khan is an advocate of the passionate and curious mind. He believes that all humans are innately equipped to be endlessly exploratory, to ask questions, and to be fascinated by the world and other minds around them. His goal is to foster readers' passion and curiosity.

Printed in Poland
by Amazon Fulfillment
Poland Sp. z o.o., Wrocław

72304545R00065